Haunted Western Pennsylvania

D1518436

Haunted
Western Pennsylvania

Ghosts and Strange Phenomena of Pittsburgh, Erie, and the Laurel Highlands

Patty A. Wilson

Illustrations by Marc Radle

STACKPOLE
BOOKS

Published by
STACKPOLE BOOKS
5067 Ritter Road
Mechanicsburg, PA 17055
www.stackpolebooks.com

Printed in the United States of America

Distributed by NATIONAL BOOK NETWORK

FIRST EDITION

Cover design by Tessa J. Sweigert

Library of Congress Cataloging-in-Publication Data

Wilson, Patty A.
  Haunted western Pennsylvania : ghosts and strange phenomena of Pittsburgh, Erie, and the Laurel Highlands / Patty A. Wilson. — FIRST EDITION.
     pages cm
  Includes bibliographical references.
  ISBN 978-0-8117-1197-5 (pbk.)
  1. Haunted places—Pennsylvania—Pittsburgh Region. 2. Haunted places—Pennsylvania—Erie Region. 3. Haunted places—Pennsylvania—Laurel Highlands. 4. Ghosts—Pennsylvania—Pittsburgh Region. 5. Ghosts—Pennsylvania—Erie Region. 6. Ghosts—Pennsylvania—Laurel Highlands. I. Title.
  BF1472.U6W5583 2013
  133.109748'8—dc23
                              2013021002

Contents

Introduction

WESTERN PENNSYLVANIA'S HISTORY IS A MICROCOSM OF THE NATION'S history. The bravery, passions, and hard work that built America are exemplified in Western Pennsylvania's past. Early settlers came to the area to begin a new life, bringing their hopes and dreams and the ability to persevere. It is little wonder that some of those folks have never left Western Pennsylvania.

This book on hauntings and paranormal phenomena in Western Pennsylvania is separated into three sections: the Pittsburgh Region, Erie and Northwest Pennsylvania, and the Laurel Highlands. Each section has terrifying and touching tales spanning more than two hundred years. The ghostly goings-on range from the traumatized spirits of murdered young women to an elegant hotel haunted by an equally elegant spirit. So I welcome you to the strange, bizarre, and haunted world of Western Pennsylvania.

Region

PITTSBURGH AND ITS ENVIRONS EXEMPLIFY BOTH THE COSMOPOLITAN AND the most impoverished extremes of life. The wealthy grew richer while many others toiled in poverty. The stories of this region include the tale of one of the finest hotels in the world—the Omni William Penn Hotel—and the story of Liberace, who was healed by a ghostly nun. The story of the Green Man is a unique part of the fabric of Western Pennsylvania, covering the whole region. Relax and read on, but make sure to keep the lights on.

Pittsburgh Playhouse

Ghosts and theaters seem to go together. A disproportionate number of recorded ghostly tales are set in these large performance centers. Many people scoff at the notion of a haunted theater and say that theater folk are an imaginative lot, but there are some theaters that are so haunted the stories seem undeniable. The Pittsburgh Playhouse, which has housed multiple theaters and now holds three, is such a place. Actors, patrons, maintenance workers, and other visitors have experienced numerous ghosts there through the years.

One of the most famous ghosts from the theater is a once-famous Pittsburgh actor, John Johns. Johns performed at the theater for a decade starting in 1950 and was quickly hailed as the preeminent performer there. He favored the restaurant in the basement of the Rockwell Theater, and one night while dining he suddenly collapsed with a heart attack. Johns was carried to Dressing Room 7. He was in the room for only a few seconds before he died. Since then, performers assigned to Dressing Room 7 have reported hearing phantom footsteps walking around the room. The steps follow them as far as the doorway, where they suddenly stop. Staff and patrons alike have had experiences with John Johns. He has been seen sitting alone in the Hamlet Street Theater after a show empties out and disappears when staff members approach him. Some patrons have seen him in the seat beside them and only realize who he is when they later see his photograph in the lobby.

The Hamlet Street Theater, now the dressing room area, has been home to other spirits as well. A Woman in White was reported there, gracefully walking across the balcony. She has also been seen in the Upstairs Theater, which was once home to a brothel. No one knows if she was once a lady of the evening or a young actress returning to where she had lived her dreams. Today the Upstairs Theater is used for storage, so she hasn't been reported in recent years.

Another spirit who haunts the Hamlet Street Theater is known as "Weeping Eleanor." Eleanor has never appeared to anyone, but she has certainly made herself well known. People report hearing a woman sobbing in one of the dressing rooms late at night. The sound is so heart-rending that those who hear it often try to find the poor woman to comfort her. Though they follow the sound, they never find the woman.

Long before the Hamlet Street section was built, there were row houses on the same ground. One night one of the houses caught fire. The fire quickly spread and fear rippled through the houses. People poured out of the houses and milled around as the fire department arrived to fight the blaze. It seemed as though everyone was accounted for; however, the next day the body of a young woman named Eleanor and her little daughter were found in one of the houses. They had been trapped and died there. It is said that late at night Eleanor returns to the site of her former home to weep for the little daughter that she could not save from the fire.

Another ghost at the theater is unique to western Pennsylvania. There is a hideous, green-skinned man who stalks the prop area at the theater. He has been nicknamed "Gorgeous George," and he is seen behind the props, pounding on the window of the costume shop. One night an actress was in the costume shop when the pounding began. She looked up at the window and gasped in shock. The horrid green man grinned back, waved, and faded out.

In 1974, a group of college students decided it would be fun to hold a séance on Halloween night in the Rockwell Theater, which had once been a Jewish synagogue. The students were locked in the theater and told that they couldn't call out as the telephone system was shut down for the night as usual. The kids set up their Ouija board on the stage, lit candles, and began the séance. They called out to the spirits, but the planchette on the board remained still. The only light in the theater was on stage, and so it took a few minutes for their eyes to adjust to the darkness beyond the light.

Then one of the students began to think that someone or something was moving in the back of the theater. Everyone strained to look and they all saw it pacing back and forth in the back of the room. Suddenly, the figure moved forward and they could see that it was a man in red. His face was painted as a scowling clown, and as they watched, it began to glow. They could see that he had a strange expression on his face. As he continued forward, he began to levitate. The figure shot sideways and literally began bouncing off the walls. He shot upward to the ceiling and from wall to wall. The phones that they had been told were turned off began to ring. It sounded like every phone in the building began ringing at the same time. The kids stared in horror because every seat in the auditorium was suddenly filled with ghostly patrons dressed in clothing from approximately 1900.

The students broke and ran. They found a way out and left their Ouija board behind. In the morning, they contacted the management to tell them about what had happened. Others have since seen the figure in red who bounced off the walls. He has become known as the "Bouncing Red Meanie" (or "Loony"). Through research, the theater found out that there was a type of clown called a Red Meanie that often performed in theaters in the early years of the 1900s.

The Pittsburgh Playhouse is a world class theater. It boasts wonderful actors and plays . . . and also some of the best hauntings in western Pennsylvania.

National Aviary

Pittsburgh is a beautiful city filled with museums, historical sites, and wonderful tourist attractions. Among the many must-visit spots is the National Aviary. Located at 700 Arch Street, the National Aviary was one of the first zoos in the nation to have free-flight rooms, where visitors actually enter the habitat of wild birds and view them as they would in nature, rather than in cages. The domed rooms give the birds an opportunity to live much as they do in the wild. Currently, there are approximately six hundred birds in the aviary with two hundred species represented, including rare and endangered birds. The National Aviary offers many educational opportunities and programs for those interested in birds and birding. They also have a very successful breeding program that is helping to keep nearly extinct species alive.

The National Aviary, however, sits upon storied land. It was once the site of the Western State Penitentiary, the smaller, western sister of the notorious Eastern State Penitentiary. The Western State Penitentiary was not nearly as violent as her eastern counterpart and probably housed less violent criminals. The prison was built in 1826 and ran until 1880, when a newer, larger prison was built a few blocks away.

In 1863, the prison was pressed into service as prisoner-of-war housing for Confederate soldiers and officers. The prisoners were well treated by the standards of the day, but some records indicate that there were a few deaths during that time. It is said that six men died of injuries related to battles they had fought in prior to being captured. One man also supposedly died while trying to escape. The prisoners were held there approximately one year and were removed in 1864.

Once the prison was abandoned in 1880, it was eventually torn down. The citizens of Pittsburgh decided to use the land to build a conservatory, which caught fire in the late 1920s during a gas explosion. The ruins of the conservatory were removed, and in 1952, the city of Pittsburgh rebuilt the conservatory, and this time added birds to the building as part of the displays.

People began to come for the birds more than the plants, and by the 1980s the conservatory became an aviary. As funding for the facility began to dry up, the aviary faced the prospect of closing. A group of concerned citizens created Save the Aviary, Inc., to raise funds. The group was successful, and in 1992, the conservatory became a private organization. In the 1990s, the facility added other buildings. The federal government gave it the honorary status of National Aviary.

For many years, people have been having strange paranormal experiences in the building; however, the episodes were kept quiet for some time. People have long reported shadowy figures that dart around the building early in the day and late in the evening. Some staffers have heard phantom footsteps through the halls and in the living areas for the birds. On multiple occasions, the birds have reacted to something that the keepers could not see. Staffers have reported that birds in a quiet area at the far end of an enclosure have been suddenly roused from sleep. Then the birds farther down the hall begin reacting, too, as if something was walking down the hall frightening the birds.

Another phenomenon often experienced by staffers and maintenance workers is the sound of pounding or banging in the basement. When they check on it, the source is never found.

Staffers often report the feeling of being watched or the sense that they are not alone. They talk about being followed as they work and feeling as though someone is keeping tabs on them.

One staffer said that early one morning she was preparing food for the birds. She usually listened to the radio in the kitchen while she worked, but that morning she hadn't bothered with it. While the staffer worked at the counter near the radio, it suddenly flipped itself on. She froze as the thing blared to life. As she stared at it, the dial began to move up and down, as if a ghostly hand was turning it and looking for a station.

There have been visitors who claim to have seen apparitions in Confederate uniforms in the halls and the atrium. It is believed that some of the spirits there are those of former Confederate prisoners of war. Neither these spirits nor those of other prisoners at this site indicate that they mean any harm. They seem to enjoy the birds and staff who now inhabit the site. The National Aviary is a peaceful place, and even the spirits there seem intent upon keeping it that way.

Liberace's Visitor

Pianist, singer, and flamboyant star of a wildly popular syndicated TV variety show that began broadcasting in 1952, Liberace was one of the highest paid entertainers of his day. He dressed in flashy clothes, furs, and jewels, and appeared with his trademark candelabra on a grand piano. On his show, he spoke to the viewers as if they were in the room and became an instant hit with women.

In 1963, Liberace agreed to be booked for a sixteen-day run at the Holiday House, a nightclub on Route 22 in Monroeville. Opening night, November 23, he was preparing for the concert when he noticed that one of his costumes was smudged with dirt. He later described in his posthumously published autobiography, *The Wonderful Private World of Liberace*, that he was unable to find anyone to clean the costume, so he went out and bought a gallon of cleaning fluid to get the dirt out. The fluid, unfortunately, contained the deadly chemical carbon tetrachloride. He cleaned the costume and then lay down to take a nap while it dried.

Liberace awoke and prepared for the concert, which was sold out, but he didn't feel well. Believing that "the show must go on," he dressed in his first costume and stepped out to perform. He glittered on the stage in his gold jacket and joked with the crowd before settling at the piano to begin the first number.

After the song was over, Liberace smiled and joked again with the crowd. He bowed and said, "Maybe you folks will excuse me, because I'd like to get into something more spectacular." With that, he left the stage and a local singer took over. Liberace managed to get backstage before he began vomiting. He struggled to clean up and get back in place to begin his concert again and managed to perform for another hour before he stood, blew out the candles on his piano, and walked off stage. When he got backstage, he collapsed. Immediately, he was rushed to Columbia Hospital, but they did not have the facilities to help him, and sent him on to St. Francis Hospital in Lawrenceville.

At St. Francis Hospital, doctors isolated the problem—he was dying from uremic poisoning because of exposure to toxic cleaning fluid. Liberace's kidneys were shutting down and fluid was building up in his body tissue. It was a desperate situation. He was placed on an artificial kidney machine, but then the doctors had to broach a terrible subject with Liberace. He was dying. His chance of survival was only about 30 percent.

An expert was called in, but no one held out much hope for Liberace's survival. He suffered through the night and the next day. There was not much more that the staff at the hospital could do but keep him comfortable. On the second night, Liberace was sedated to ease his pain. It was on that night that he would receive an unexpected visitor.

Liberace later wrote in his autobiography, "A very young and lovely nun wearing a white habit came to see me late one night, when I was very near death. She said she was going to pray to St. Anthony for me, and he would make me well."

The next day, Liberace's kidneys began to function again. It was a miracle and he was told that he would make a full recovery. The doctors were puzzled and pleased by the change in fortune for their patient.

Liberace confided his story to the nuns who nursed him. He wrote, "I described the nun to the Mother Superior at the hospital and asked who she was. The Mother Superior said, 'There are no nuns in the hospital who wear white habits.'" The nuns on duty that night did not recall such a nun having been on the floor. No one but Liberace had seen her.

Throughout his life, Liberace pondered exactly what happened to him in the hospital in Pittsburgh. He gave credit to the doctors for saving his life, but he also wrote about the nun in the white habit and continued to talk about her. He chose to believe that she was sent to guide him in his moment of crisis. Liberace shared the story publically many times in his life, and each time he asserted that he believed that the nun had been real and was sent to bring him a miracle.

The Omni William Penn Hotel

The Omni William Penn Hotel was built in 1916 by Pittsburgh steel magnate and financier Henry Clay Frick. Frick spared no expense in the building of the hotel and his attention to detail still shows. Brass handrails in the elevators, grand murals, and sweeping Old World charm set the William Penn Hotel apart. When the hotel opened, it was dubbed the "Grande Dame," and that moniker still holds true. Everything about the William Penn speaks of the luxury and grace of a bygone era. The twenty-three-floor building offers 596 elegantly decorated guest rooms, including thirty-eight suites, two conference centers, flexible meeting spaces, five dining areas, a spa, jewelry store, beauty salon, and gift shop.

The William Penn has been part of the fabric of Pittsburgh ever since it opened its doors. Financiers, railroad moguls, businessmen, movie stars, and many others have graced the building. Every American president since Theodore Roosevelt has visited the hotel.

The William Penn also serves as a part of the community. It is famous for hosting weddings. The staff talks about their work serving bridal couples with great enthusiasm and fondness. One staffer who gave his first name, Cory, talked about families who choose the hotel for all of their wedding needs. He explained that he has seen families who come back for generations. He expressed how much he enjoys helping to make the bridal couple's dreams come true. Cory certainly knows a great deal about the subject because he has been working at the William Penn Hotel for thirty-one years in catering sales.

Cory had long heard stories that the hotel was haunted, but he never thought much about it because in his many years there he had never encountered any spirits. He had seen shadows flitting along and figures that faded almost before the mind could register them, but he brushed them off. He also encountered disembodied footsteps and a feeling of not being alone, but had no concrete evidence of a haunting, until one night when the stories suddenly took on a new meaning for him.

Cory shared his very personal experiences publically for the first time. One night he was working a catering job, and by 9:30 P.M. he had finished up his work. He returned to his office to gather his things and leave. As he walked down the hallway to his office, he knew that he was alone on the seventeenth floor. It was late and the other offices were dark. He gathered his belongings, stepped back into the hall, and locked the door to his office. It was then that he heard the elevator stop on his floor.

At first he thought it was a coworker getting off the elevator, but he heard nothing. He suddenly felt compelled to go look. He went down the hall toward the elevator and rounded the corner in time to see a woman in a white dress walking away. He could not see her face, but he could clearly see she was slim and in a long, lacy dress from about the 1930s, with white shoes. He hurried forward, but when he rounded the corner she was gone. Suddenly, Cory realized that he had just seen the famous Lady in White who had been reported throughout the hotel—and usually in or near the elevators. Cory was not frightened, but rather amazed by his sighting.

Cory related another story. On Halloween 2010, a private group was having a Halloween party in the hotel and they had hired a psychic to divine the spirits there. They had heard stories about the hotel being haunted and were titillated by them. They had heard that the upper two floors of the hotel had housed college coeds during the 1960s and 1970s. According to the tale told on the internet, there was a murder on the dormitory floors at that time. Ever since then, people have reported voices and the giggling of a girl. (The story of the murder is not supported by any facts; however, students from a local university once did have housing on the top two floors.)

The party organizers wanted the psychic to take groups of people up to the top levels to look for ghosts. While the hotel deemed that a possible safety risk, they did agree that the psychic could walk through the two floors as long as she was accompanied by someone from the hotel staff. Cory agreed to go along with the psychic.

The psychic did not find any spirits on the two top floors, and Cory was heartened by that because he knew that the gory tale was not true. The woman seemed honest and sincere, so he decided to ask her to walk through another area that he had heard staff say was haunted.

Cory took the psychic to the second floor human resources office area that was then under construction. He knew that the area was said to be haunted by a former employee who had worked for the hotel for twenty years and then became ill and could not fulfill her job, although the hotel kept her on because she had been such a good employee. After the woman died, they hired another person to take over her job. The new employee was given her office and all of her old furniture. He later confided to other staffers that a woman kept appearing in his office. He described her as very proper and dressed in a nice suit. She had a scarf around her neck and her blond hair was cut in a bob. The woman was seen throughout his office, but mostly near his desk. He would come to learn that he had perfectly described the lady who had once held his job.

Cory led the psychic to the gutted section and stood there quietly. The psychic acknowledged that the area was haunted. She described the woman with short blond hair and said she was very fond of working and was very businesslike in dress and demeanor. She also said that the woman wore a scarf around her neck. Cory recognized the description immediately. Then the psychic walked across the empty floor and pointed to an area. "Here," she said, "is where her desk once sat." There were no clues as to the position of the desk in the gutted room; however, Cory felt a thrill of excitement because the woman was accurate. The woman's desk had occupied the very spot she indicated.

Darlene is a catering manager who has worked for the hotel for thirty-three years. She loves her job and the hotel's grandeur. She spoke about her singular encounter with a ghost at the hotel.

One evening, Darlene and a coworker were in the hotel lobby waiting for the elevator. When the doors opened, they saw a woman in a white flowing gown standing there. They stepped inside and suddenly looked at each other. No one had gotten off the elevator, but the woman in the white gown suddenly vanished. Darlene looked at her companion and asked, "Did you see someone in here?" Her companion confirmed that he had seen a woman in white clothes. They talked a moment and both agreed that the woman's clothing looked vintage, like something from the 1940s. They realized that they had seen the hotel's famous Lady in White. No one knows the story of this woman who lurks near the elevators, but she is the most often glimpsed ghostly presence in the building.

Staffers all know the stories of voices calling out when people are alone. The desk staff has heard excited guests explain that they had been awakened in the night to find someone standing by their beds watching them and then fading away. Other guests have heard disembodied footsteps following them down halls. Still others describe the feeling that they are not alone; however, they say they do not feel a sense of fear. The fictional gruesome tales of murder should be laid to rest because the ghosts at the William Penn Hotel don't seem to hail from any tragic event. Whoever the ghosts are, they seem to linger not to frighten, but rather to enjoy the hotel itself. It is truly a grand and haunted place.

Flaming Scalps

Before there was a city of Pittsburgh, and even before Fort Pitt existed, a man and his brother paddled down a creek in the area looking for a place to settle. Their surname was Chartier, and they were hoping to bring their family to the New World to build a new life.

The Chartiers settled and built a cabin on property they claimed by "tomahawk rights." That meant they claimed a plot of ground by marking their initials with a tomahawk in the trees near a water source. Tomahawk claims were not legally recognized by the British government, but they were accepted by many of the natives and early white settlers. Approximately a year later, one Chartier brother brought his wife and two children to the settlement.

The family settled in and Chartier and his brother shared the hard work of developing the land. Chartier's wife cared for her two small children and cooked for the family. In the late fall, the brothers felt a push to get meat in for the winter and began hunting in earnest. Their trips took longer and longer as they wandered farther away looking for big game.

One afternoon the brothers were making their way home from a long hunting trip. They were packing meat, which made the going slow. They noticed smoke in the distance and realized that it was too much to have come from the cabin chimney. They hurried as fast as they could and soon made it to the cabin site. What met their shocked eyes was a grisly scene. Chartier's wife and two children had been brutally murdered and scalped. Their mutilated bodies horrified the men. The cabin was a smoldering ruin and their lives were changed forever.

The two brothers realized that they were in danger, too. Quickly, they buried their dead and then pinned a note on birch bark for others to find. It told of the tragedy that had befallen them. The brothers said that they were tracking the murderers and were going to seek vengeance for the deaths.

Trappers eventually found the letter and carried it to the authorities. The Chartiers were never heard from again. Other settlers claimed the cleared land and built cabins in the area where the poor little family had been killed.

Eventually, the new settlers began to talk about hearing terrifying screams. It was believed that the poor mother and her children were reliving their last moments alive. Folks claimed to see death lights flitting around over the site of the tragedy. The three lights would flicker out when people drew near. Others, however, have seen a much darker sight. There are some people who claim to have seen the golden flickering of three bloody scalps moving through the darkness. The scalps seem to glow with fire but are not consumed. Blood is said to drip from scalps and it does not dissipate when the scalps fade away.

The Crow Sisters

When Jacob Crow came to America in 1765, he knew that he was embarking on an adventure. He must have realized that it was dangerous, but he placed his faith in God and trudged onward. A new life did not come easy. He came indentured and had to work off his passage before he and his family could begin their lives. He gathered his wife and eleven children and made for western Pennsylvania in the area of today's Greene County. There he found a good stand of timber, fresh water, and land flat enough to be tilled one day. He had four sons and seven daughters, and he knew that he would have to plant a good homestead deep in this new land to provide for their future.

In 1789, three of his sons were attacked by natives while hunting in what is today West Virginia. One died and the other two barely escaped with their lives. All around them, Jacob saw how painful the struggle could become. Neighbors were murdered, burned out of their homes, or carried off, but his big, hearty brood of children flourished. They were part of the mountains and the woods that surrounded them. At their homestead they felt safe—as long as they were careful.

On May 1, 1791, four of Jacob's teenage girls asked to go visiting an elderly couple a few miles away. Jacob had made the journey himself in the past and felt confident the girls would be fine, so he allowed them to make the trip.

Excited, the girls started off. About a mile and a half from the homestead they noticed something in the creek. They lingered at the edge of the water talking and laughing. It was a fine warm day and the cool near the water felt good. The place was a scenic spot with tall pines, towering mountains, and the whisper of the water to lull them into a false sense of peace. As they paused, their youngest brother, Michael, came along riding bareback on a horse that had strayed away earlier.

Michael stopped to talk to his sisters, and while they chatted, the horse suddenly got skittish. It pranced and reared as if sensing something. The boy looked around but saw nothing. Still, Michael became uneasy and attempted to persuade his thirteen-year-old sister to climb up behind him and go home with him. She would not be swayed, however, for she was enjoying the camaraderie of being with the older girls. At last, Michael left them and rode home.

Only moments after the brother left, two Indians and a white man named Spicer appeared among the boulders and then advanced on the girls, waving tomahawks. The men shouted out in a menacing way and the girls fell silent in fear. They knew Spicer's story. His family had been massacred when he was but a tiny child. He and his one sibling were spared and they had been raised by the natives. He knew no other life.

Quickly, the men gathered up the girls and made signs to indicate that they wanted silence. They forced the girls to march up from the creek ford to a place where there was a fallen tree. The girls were forced to sit there. The one native ran off in the direction their brother had taken. The other native and Spicer sat on the log like bookends, holding the hands of the girls nearest and demanding information in broken English. How many settlers were in the area? What armaments did they have? The questions went on and on. The girls answered as their eyes darted for any avenue of escape.

After what seemed a long time, the other native returned. The men spoke in the guttural language of their tribe, and then they looked down upon the girls. The girls had been raised in the wilderness. They knew what was to come. The two natives stood the girls up and split them into pairs. The sisters in each pair clasped hands, and then the natives grabbed their locked hands in an iron grip.

With stunning suddenness, the men swung their tomahawks and struck one girl in the head. There were screams and one of the sisters, Christina, broke the grip and ran. She was pursued and struck on the head by a gun butt. She fell to the ground, wounded by the tomahawk and stunned by the gun. The native turned back to help murder the other girls. He planned to return to this one later to kill and scalp her. The girl realized that she had a chance. She jumped up and ran as fast as she could. In her condition she was unable to tell if she was being pursued. She burst into the house and collapsed. It only took one look to see what had happened. The family began gathering up things to flee. Jacob questioned Christina and from her answers he knew that he could no longer help his other girls. He gathered his remaining children, including Michael, and fled for the block house at Lindsey's Mills, nearly twenty miles distant.

At first light the next day, a party from the block house arrived at the creek ford to see if the girls were alive. Two were clearly dead. The third girl was badly wounded and had been left for dead. She had been unconscious most of the time, but had been driven by thirst to the water's edge sometime before first light. Upon seeing her brother Michael, she cast defeated eyes at him. "Why did you not come sooner," she whispered. "Why did you not come?"

The girl had been scalped and her skull was opened. A doctor tried to save her, but she died three days after the attack. The first two girls to die were buried in a common grave on the homestead, and the third sister was buried days later alongside them. Two unmarked fieldstones stand sentinel over the graves.

The scene of the attack is remembered still today. Occasionally, hikers and history buffs report hearing the horrible cries of the girls or the sound of the laughter the girls shared shortly before their lives were brutally taken from them. Others have seen the girls along the water's edge briefly before they fade away.

The Hoodoo Engine Bad Luck 1313

Railroading is filled with unusual tales and strange stories of bad luck trains abound. Perhaps the strangest is about a hoodoo train from the Pennsylvania Railroad (PRR), which was known for many years as the largest and finest railroad system in the world.

There has long been a superstition that the number 13 is a bad luck number, and when the PRR's Engine 1313 came off the line, there were those who muttered darkly that nothing good could come of it. The PRR administration, however, was not superstitious, so they did not change the number.

Engine 1313 went on the line early in 1888. On its maiden voyage, disaster struck when two children were killed by the train. Although the engine was found to be in perfect working order, it again met with disaster in mid-summer when it plunged off a railroad bridge at Latrobe, killing twelve people, including the engineer and fireman. Ten others were badly injured in the accident. Only a month later, Engine 1313 collided with another train near the town of Manor and seriously injured several people, including the new fireman. Several cars derailed during the accident as well.

The engine was once again inspected but nothing was found to be wrong with it. It was put on the line again, and only a few weeks later the boiler blew while the train climbed a steep mountain. The fireman was blown out of the car and badly injured.

A new boiler system was then installed and the train went back on the line. By now, the PRR had begun to hear rumblings from the men, but a train engine was an expensive investment and no one was going to let a perfectly good engine sit because of a lot of superstitious gossip. For several months the engine seemed to work fine, but one day when arriving at Manor Station its brakes failed and it once more rammed another train. The fireman for the run was injured.

The PRR pulled the train off the line and went over the brakes again. The mechanics had heard stories that brake failure on Engine 1313 caused other accidents, but they found nothing wrong. Everything was upgraded and the train went back on the line.

Only a couple weeks later, the engine failed to stop at a station when the engineer applied the brakes. It came to rest only after striking and killing three people. Once more, the PRR's mechanics went over the train, but there was nothing wrong with the engine.

A few weeks after it was placed back on the rails, it was going through Sang Hollow when the oil can suddenly exploded, badly burning the fireman and the engineer. That was the last straw for those who had to make runs on Engine 1313. It was reported in multiple newspapers that those employees asked the company to pull it from the rails. They were afraid to work on the engine. From that point, Engine 1313 was never run again.

The Black Cross

The 1918 influenza pandemic infected five hundred million people worldwide and killed more than fifty million. Several factors came into play to make this the worst flu season in modern times. First, the closing of World War I meant that soldiers were returning to their home countries from around the world. Travel had been curtailed because of the war, but suddenly many people were traveling again. Soldiers who had become infected or exposed to the flu carried the virus home, where it quickly spread. This flu was also particularly virulent.

Pennsylvania was impacted by the flu just like every other part of the world. In some towns, more than half the population succumbed to the disease. There are accounts of entire families dying from the flu. The first cases were traced to January 1918, and by September of that year it reached Butler County, bringing down hundreds of people by the following month. It was a true medical emergency and the authorities called for immediate burial of the dead to help curb the spread of the disease. In many places, mass graves were created to quickly get rid of the dead.

In West Winfield Township the bodies were adding up rapidly. Businesses that required labor were hotspots for the spread of the disease. Near the Armstrong County border, several companies and some small mining camps were struck with the virus. Many of those employed in both places were recent immigrants who had no families to claim their bodies when they died. A makeshift cemetery was set up to receive their bodies. Because of the quantity of bodies to be interred, each grave was said to contain around five bodies, but several of the grave diggers later asserted that as many as twenty people had been buried in some graves. There were at least three hundred people in the area who died of the influenza. No one kept count of how many were buried in mass graves, but the number is significant.

After the epidemic eased, a local priest, Father Jeremiah O'Callahan, stepped forward to say that the poor dead immigrants deserved a proper funeral service. He had a large wooden cross fashioned from railroad ties, and it was installed above the mass gravesite. The railroad ties that fashioned the cross were dipped in creosote that had blackened them. Father O'Callahan held a graveside mass for the dead and gave their hasty burial some dignity.

The mass grave and the heavy black cross became a part of local lore. The cross itself has rotted away through the years, and today at the site there is a historical marker and a small wooden cross carved into a billet of wood. People occasionally leave wreaths and flowers in memory of the dead. Legends grew up around the site and people have talked about hearing howls coming from the graves and the sounds of infants crying and people talking. Strange winds are said to blow through the spot, and some people report a feeling of being watched. If troubled spirits remain active, then it is easy to understand why this site is considered haunted.

Sad Louisa

Arthur St. Clair was a British soldier in the French and Indian War who settled in Pennsylvania. He became a major general in the Continental Army during the American Revolution and after the war served briefly as the president of the Continental Congress. He was a man who made decisions that affected the nation, but he died poor and living with his daughter Louisa. St. Clair had three daughters and two sons whom he loved dearly, but Louisa was said to be his favorite.

There are no portraits of Louisa, but she is often described as beautiful, headstrong, and willful. She could hunt, ride, shoot a bow, and traverse the woods better than most men. She also was sent to finishing school near Philadelphia to master the skills of a lady. She could dance, dressed divinely, and yet always did the unexpected and spoke her mind. Louisa grew up between two worlds, living in the frontier in Ligonier Valley and participating in high society.

At the age of eighteen, Louisa was in school near Philadelphia, where she first laid eyes upon Joseph Michael Brandt. Michael, as she would affectionately call him, was the son of Joseph Brandt, the renowned Mohawk leader within the Six Nations of the Iroquois Confederacy.

Joseph Michael Brandt was studying in Philadelphia and was known to be quite a scholar. He was educated, spoke several languages, and wrote in three languages. He was also a very handsome young man who wore a mixture of native and American clothing along with his native jewelry, headband, and traditional head dressing.

The young couple allegedly met at a dance and instantly became friends. They had a great deal in common for they came from the same area and enjoyed many of the same things. It is said that Michael and Louisa became romantically involved and there are letters that could be read that way. They were always careful, but they both held great esteem for each other and expressed it in many of the letters; however, their fathers were on different sides of the French and Indian War and their interlude was brief.

Joseph Michael Brandt returned home to assist his father as they struggled to keep their traditional homeland. Louisa joined her father back in Ligonier and traveled with him into the Ohio frontier to negotiate with the native people. Her father became the first governor of the Northwest Territory and settled his family in Marietta, the capital of the territory.

In the Northwest Territory, Louisa entertained a friend by the name of Marianne Navarre. Her father introduced his daughter and her guest to a young French-Canadian officer, Major Jean-François Hamtramck. The governor hoped to spark a romance between his headstrong daughter and the young officer, but Louisa was not interested in him; however, Marianne Navarre and young Hamtramck soon became involved. When St. Clair found out that Hamtramck was secretly courting his house guest, he became incensed.

At the same time, Michael Brandt had arrived at Duncan Falls with two hundred warriors and some of their families. Brandt had refused to visit the subject of peace or war at Fort Harmar because he did not trust being at the mercy of the military on their own ground. Instead, he moved down the river to Duncan Falls, and then sent a runner to inform Governor St. Clair that he desired to begin the treaty preliminaries at that site. St. Clair found the whole procedure suspect and told the runner that he would send his reply back to the natives by ranger in a day or two.

St. Clair waffled back and forth about his decision. He was afraid that this was a plot to abduct him, but he had no specific proof. As he struggled with his decision, he confided his fears to Louisa, who had come to keep her father company. Finally, her father decided to agree to the meeting and he penned a letter to that effect. He called in a ranger named Hamilton (Ham) Kerr and entrusted him with the letter.

Louisa begged her father for permission to deliver the letter. She had heard that Michael Brandt was at the falls and she longed to see him again. Her father was appalled at the notion of sending his young daughter into the enemy camp. He refused her request and forbid her to consider the idea further.

Louisa went to her room feeling petulant and resentful. Michael was mere miles away and she could have delivered the letter and seen him. She rode as well as the men at the fort and she was not afraid. Louisa was resentful of the fact that girls were not allowed to have any adventure and fun at all.

She bounced off her bed and dug out the native clothing she had purchased months ago on a lark. She shook out her deerskin dress, leggings, and boots. She smiled to herself and went to bed. At first light she would set out for Michael's camp and bring word of her father's decision. She would have to be careful so that Ham Kerr did not intercept her, but that only added to the fun. As satisfied as a kitten who had stolen some milk, she settled in to sleep.

Early that morning, she donned her clothes and made her way to the stable where she threw a blanket over the back of a horse, grabbed the horse's mane, and jumped onto its back. She had ridden bareback before and quickly guided the horse out of the stable and through a back gate so that she was not noticed. She turned her horse toward the river and rode toward the falls.

Ranger Kerr meanwhile had just left the fort as well. He had waited until daylight so that he could see to protect himself from attack. He also turned toward the river and started for the falls. He noticed tracks as he neared Waterford and decided to reconnoiter before going further. He tethered his horse and climbed a bluff for a better vantage point. He was shocked to see Louisa St. Clair riding bareback with a gun slung across her shoulder.

Ham slid down the hill in his haste to catch up with the girl, mounted his horse, and gave chase. Louisa caught sight of him and threw back her head, laughing. It was pure joy to be racing Ham and heading for Duncan Falls and Michael.

Ham caught up to Louisa and slowed her mount by grabbing its reins. He demanded to know what Louisa was doing and was shocked to find out that she was set to do the task her father had commanded of him. He knew that he could not deter Louisa, and so he agreed to allow her to accompany him. They rode on and rested fitfully that night.

Louisa stole the letter out of Ham's bag early in the morning and rode off before he awakened. She rode into the camp at Duncan Falls, fearlessly shouting, "I will speak to Joseph Brandt!"

Within seconds the Native Americans had surrounded her and pulled her from her horse. She continued to shout for Joseph Michael Brandt as she was shoved roughly face first into the ground. The crowd howled and whooped at the girl and this noise drew the young leader's attention.

Joseph Michael Brandt hurried toward the crowd. He was dressed in his traditional clothes and looked regal. The crowd parted and to his amazement he was once more face to face with Louisa St. Clair. He smiled, and Louisa flashed a grin back at him.

"Noble warrior," she said boldly. "I have risked my life for this interview." She gave him her father's missive and asked him for safe passage back to her father, reminding him of their time in Philadelphia.

Brandt's eyes twinkled. "Louisa, I do not need reminding. My heart has always been with you." Brandt took Louisa's hand and helped her up. He informed the warriors gathered there that this young woman was under his protection and she was not a captive.

He pointed out her bravery in riding into the enemy camp and told his men to honor her for that. "Louisa, I will take you home," he informed her.

Brandt called for his horse and provisions. After Louisa had rested a while, they began the journey back to her father's home. He personally delivered Louisa back to her father's front door. It was not a popular move, because his warriors would have preferred to hold her captive for ransom. The settlers at the fort, likewise, were not pleased that Brandt had dared to come among them.

What transpired upon that journey can only be guessed at, but St. Clair offered Brandt the hospitality of his home in return for bringing back his recalcitrant daughter, and Brandt asked St. Clair to bless a marriage between him and his daughter. Brandt and Louisa told St. Clair of their first meeting and how they had maintained a relationship. They confessed that they loved each other and wanted to be together.

St. Clair heard them out, but then he refused to bless the union. He reasoned with them that it was an impossible love. Brandt owed allegiance to his people and Louisa was the daughter of the man being paid to protect the settlers from Brandt's people. Louisa would be forced to give up her family to go with Brandt and she was not equipped to live as a native. It was not possible. Louisa did not take this well and was even more shocked when her father declared that she could not marry Brandt for another reason—St. Clair wanted her to marry Major Hamtramck.

Hamtramck was not privy to that information, and when Marianne was sent back home he was unaware that it was because St. Clair thought she was interfering with the match he wanted between his willful daughter and Hamtramck. The major did not marry Louisa, though. He would marry someone else.

Michael Brandt was given safe passage back to Duncan Falls. He would go with his fellow leaders to Fort Harmar for the signing of the official treaty in January 1789. He did not participate in the negotiations, but he did stay for the feast and to see Louisa again. Once more he sought out St. Clair and asked to marry Louisa. Again, St. Clair refused him.

In the fall of 1791, Michael Brandt successfully led a band of Chippewa in battle against St. Clair and his men. On that day, Brandt ordered his warriors to shoot the horse out from under St.

Clair, but not harm him. St. Clair lost four horses that day, but he was unharmed. Michael Brandt sent word that he had spared St. Clair in honor of his undying love for Louisa.

Losing the battle to Brandt cost St. Clair his reputation. He took his family back to Pennsylvania and eventually lost his fortune. Louisa married Col. Samuel Robb. She and Robb had several children, but ultimately Louisa divorced Robb. She nursed her father in the last part of his life and died with the stain of being divorced—a very unusual act in that time.

As for Michael Brandt, he married twice in his lifetime. Both wives were from among his people; however, it is said that he never stopped loving Louisa. In fact, there have long been stories that he would travel to Ligonier to meet secretly with her. Whatever happened during those meetings will forever remain a mystery, but there are other stories that are also told at Fort Ligonier and its environs.

According to authors Cassandra Fell and Dr. Walter L. Powell in their book, *Ghosts and Legends of Fort Ligonier*, Louisa's spirit has lingered at Fort Ligonier. It is said she approaches people and asks if they have seen Michael. According to other stories, on certain nights two bright lights suddenly appear and come together at the fort. Those lights are believed to be the spirits of Louisa and Michael still keeping their rendezvous—even in death.

Here is an excerpt from a letter that Michael wrote to Louisa:

When stardust falls and illuminates lost trails of yesterday my moccasin prints will not rejoice beside yours in the white pathways I hope are before you. A beautiful dream dies of sadness in the heart. The spirit of Spring is now hesitation upon syllables of sorrow for our love is a mist of shadows. Teardrops tremble in my eyes and I know it is you moving within my heart. Oh that I might weep with the rain and whirl away with the clouds! No matter how hard I try to forget, you will always return to my thoughts and I know any smoke you see from a wood fire clinging to a November dawn in the Mohawk Valley will ever remind you of me. Farewell, dearest Louisa. May you ever walk in balance in the garden of the house of God.

Erie and Northwest Pennsylvania

THE NORTHWEST REGION OF PENNSYLVANIA IS A ROUGH-AND-TUMBLE place. There are stories of murderers who haunt the prison where they died, a lovely haunted church where the parishioners never want to leave, and the eerie tale of a crazed spirit who literally climbed the walls. This area was like the Wild West in the past and its ghosts are just as wild. With names like Murder Swamp and Zombie Land, the region's stories are as unique as the people who lived, died, and now haunt the area.

The Haunted Church

Rev. Robin S. Swope first brought this story to light on his blog and in his books. He has spent considerable time and effort compiling the following events. He has documented much of the haunting and has an abiding interest in St. Paul's United Evangelical Church in Erie, understandable because he serves as a minister there.

Churches have long been part of the fabric of a community. A church becomes a family of its own. Everyone knows who is kind and who has a sharp tongue. Everyone knows who is in need and who helps out. Churches are important in the lives of the congregants. People volunteer to clean, mow the grass, and complete whatever tasks that are needed. It is easy to see why many old churches are haunted. Many have deceased congregants who have come back to participate in the life of their church. St. Paul's is one such beloved church.

Passion and faith have been a driving factor since the inception of this church. In late 1850, a group of parishioners from another church splintered off to create St. Paul's. The first official meeting of the new church was in December 1850. A year later, the fledgling congregation bought ground and built a simple brick church. Erie has many large, ornate churches, but the Brick Church, as it came to be known, was distinct because of how simple it was. Through the years, the church was expanded to meet its needs, but that simple church still stands as a tribute to faith.

The church has faced many trials. The first pastor was brought up on heresy charges, but was vindicated. At one time the church bills became so difficult to pay that they sold the pews to cover the debts. There were fights over doctrine and church members splintered off, but the church remained rooted in faith and stood strong. Today St. Paul's is affiliated with the United Church of Christ.

Many in the congregation freely acknowledge the ghostly presences still lingering within the church. Several years ago, a member of the church was putting up the antique manger scene after Thanksgiving. Suddenly, a woman's voice chided, "Be careful with those." The woman turned to see who was speaking, but there was no one visible.

Perhaps one of the most haunted areas is the nursery. There are two ghosts known to haunt that area. Ruth Breene, an elderly lady who had attended the church until her death, wore a vanilla perfume that is no longer made. She was quite elderly when she passed away in the 1990s, and she was still working for the church at that time. Since her death, her high heels have been heard clicking along the hallway of the second floor education wing and down the main stairs. The scent of her perfume wafts past people moving through the building.

Ruth Breene dearly loved working in the nursery. She began that duty in the 1960s and continued for the rest of her life. On occasion, the doors to the nursery will swing open or closed on their own, and the scent of vanilla perfume drifts in the air. Those who knew Ruth Breene know that she's overseeing the nursery just as she always did.

There is another tender spirit in the nursery area as well. Nearly two decades ago, there was a teenage girl who loved to visit the nursery. She was drawn to the children and spent time there playing with the babies and toddlers. In the summer of 1994, the pastor took a van to pick up the church teens from summer camp. Sadly, upon the return trip there was an accident and the girl who liked working in the nursery died.

Ever since that time, people believe that she returns to the nursery. Doors open and close and the giggling sound of a young lady playing with children can be heard there. One of the young children the teenager favored playing with has since grown up. He claims that one day he was working on the computer in the church when he felt someone tousle his hair. He turned to see who was there, but saw no one. At that moment he got the impression of a teenage girl standing behind him.

A third spirit at the church is known by name. Clarence was a jovial fellow who enjoyed jokes, pranks, and making people smile. After he passed away, people began to report funny things. Some folks say they have been poked on their shoulders, but when they turn around, no one is there. Objects disappear and are found in odd places or are later returned to their original locations, which have been searched. Others have reported that their moods are suddenly lifted. They feel like laughing for no good reason.

The church has allowed a few paranormal investigations. They wanted to know if the haunts could be documented scientifically. A paranormal team captured a shadowy figure on tape walking through the hall toward the nursery and the office. The figure was just the trunk of a body, but it was obvious on the tape. Seconds after it passed through the hallway, the door to the church office closed without human aid. Then the torso exited the way it had entered. They captured EVP (electronic voice phenomenon) recordings, and an array of shadow people on camera. The shadow people tape brought to mind the stories of longtime congregants that had, as teens, held "lock-ins," where they would sit in the sanctuary and watch shadow people moving along the front of the church and the choir loft.

In subsequent investigations, teams caught a teenage girl's voice saying, "It's okay to die." They recorded the sounds of footsteps and doors opening and closing. They observed a rocking chair in the nursery rocking by itself, and a ball rolled itself toward an investigator who had asked for someone to play with her.

In the basement, in an area known as Fellowship Hall, lights were recorded dancing near the ceiling. Investigators recorded audio of several children laughing and playing. Objects were seen moving. Though the investigators did not know it at the time, the area where Fellowship Hall is located was once the scene of a children's Sunday school class.

On the third floor, footsteps were heard and people felt that someone was moving along near them or past them. The area had been used as living quarters for the homeless, and it is believed that at least one homeless person has returned to the church after death.

Ghostly phenomena are reported to occur with startling frequency at St. Paul's, but the spirits there have never been harmful. It is as if they are continuing their activities and watching over the living in this spirited, spiritual church.

She Who Crawls on the Wall

When the Long family moved into their new home in Erie, they did so knowing that there was something wrong with the house. The rent was far below what it should have been, and the landlord confessed to them that there had been strange things going on in the house according to the previous tenants. The Longs questioned the landlord more closely and he confessed that the house had been the scene of an attempted homicide. He explained that, in fact, several of the people he had rented to in the past had turned out to be under a great deal of stress. He indicated that on more than one occasion violence had occurred in the house and that usually the wife was the violent partner.

The Longs were more interested in their finances than local gossip, and they decided that the house would work just fine for them. The reduced rent would ease their budget, and as they were a stable couple with two small children, they saw no reason why they should worry about the past reputation of the house.

On their first walkthrough, the couple had noticed a terrible smell reminiscent of a decaying mouse. It was not strong, but it never really went away. Mrs. Long thought that a good cleaning would take care of the problem, but despite her best efforts, the smell lingered. Aside from the smell, the house was lovely and just large enough for their growing family. They settled in and unpacked.

Within days of settling in, Mrs. Long discovered that her two small children were both sleeping in her son's room. When the little children were questioned, they first said that the little girl's room was too cold. Mrs. Long began to notice that the children were right. There were strange cold spots in her daughter's room, and something about the room made her feel watched and unwelcome. She felt like she was trespassing in someone else's space. Still, the Long's decided to make their daughter sleep in her own room.

Their daughter didn't take the news well. She began to cry and told her parents that she was scared in her room. She was unable to tell them why it was scary, but Mrs. Long couldn't shake the feeling she had experienced in the room. In the end, the parents compromised and said that both children could sleep in the daughter's room for a while, until their daughter got used to it. Mrs. Long wasn't so sure it was a good idea, but like her daughter she couldn't give a good reason why.

The first night that the children stayed in the room, Mrs. Long awoke with a start at 3 A.M., when she heard her son's cries. She had barely struggled up in bed before her son burst into the room. He was terribly shaken. Tears stained his face and he was shaking. "There's something in Sissy's room!" he screamed. Just behind her son came her daughter, who was howling in fear and pain. Mrs. Long tumbled out of bed and flipped on her bedside lamp. The pool of light caused her to gasp—long red scratches ran down her daughter's face.

"Oh my God," Mrs. Long cried, sweeping her daughter up. "What happened, honey?" she soothed.

Her tiny daughter wrapped her arms around her mother's neck tightly. "The black lady on the wall saw me and she doesn't like it when I look away. She climbs along the wall and scares me. When I looked away, she scratched me, Mommy. She gets mad if you can see her but you look away!"

The children spent the rest of the night with their parents. There was no denying the scratches on her daughter's face or the terrified eyes of both children. Something had to be done before the children were further injured.

In the morning it was decided that the children would go to stay with their grandparents until the Longs could decide what to do. The only solution to the problem was to move, but that would be both expensive and time consuming. It took a few weeks to get things worked out and it was not a pleasant time.

Mrs. Long found herself sinking into a depression. She wanted to be alone all the time. She began to suffer from nightmares. She dreamed of being pursued and of being a murderer. Eventually she brought up the terrible dreams to her husband. To her relief, he didn't scoff. Instead, he said that he had been suffering through a series of nightmares, too. In his dreams, a woman wearing a veil and a long white gown seemed intent upon getting to him. He could feel that the woman was angry and that she was glaring at him. Each night she got closer and closer.

One night, Mr. Long woke up screaming, "She's here! She's here! We have to leave now!" He was wild with fear as he woke up, but waking up only made matters worse. He stared in horror at a spot on the wall. Mrs. Long only saw a hazy mist, but her husband said that there was a woman crawling along the wall, glaring at him. She knew that he could see her and she wanted him to watch her. Mr. Long kept muttering, "God, I'm awake and I still see her—I am awake!"

The Longs bolted from the bedroom and slammed the door shut on the woman who was crawling along the wall. They turned on every light in the living room and kitchen. Mrs. Long couldn't think of anything else to do but call a family friend who was studying for the ministry. She poured out the story of her house and what was going on. The minister said that he would be right over.

The minister found Mr. Long still in shock when he entered the house. He talked to Mr. Long, and then put his arm around the man as they began to pray together. Suddenly, Mr. Long pulled away. "Get it off me," he shouted, twisting around. "That thing's on me and it burns—it's burning me."

The minister increased the volume of his prayers, but Mr. Long began to buck and twist. "It's burning," he yelled in anguish. He pulled up his shirt to look. Mrs. Long could not believe her eyes. Two red marks were burned on his back where the minister's hands had been.

The minister cleansed the house that night and assured the Longs that their house was fine. For a few days, things seemed okay, but then the woman was back in Mr. Long's dreams and the feeling of anger and hatred once again permeated the house. The two cats began to growl and hiss at night at the door to the little girl's bedroom. The Longs were up most nights because of the nightmares. They missed their children terribly. Thumps and pounding noises began to come from the children's rooms.

One night the Longs began to bicker, and the bickering turned into a terrible fight. Mrs. Long had never felt such burning anger and hate. It got so bad that the neighbors called the police. The police took them out of the house and made sure that no one had been drinking—and they hadn't. Neither did they have a history of violence. That was their last night in the house. They left everything behind and never entered again. They did not dare, because on that night Mrs. Long had tried to kill her husband by strangling him. The police did not press charges because Mr. Long did not want to and one of the officers told Mrs. Long that there's something in that house that affects people badly. He'd let her go if they promised to move out.

The Longs didn't need any prodding to leave the house behind. They both knew that they had to make a complete cut with the property. They left their possessions behind and started over. They do not doubt that the house was haunted by someone or something filled with murderous hate and evil.

The Horrible Ralph Crossmire

Ralph Crossmire was a handsome young man with dark hair and penetrating eyes. He lived in Farmer's Valley, near Smethport, with his mother, Lucetta Crossmire. The two lived on a little farm left to them by Ralph's father upon his death. They lived a simple life. Lucetta participated in the Women's Christian Temperance Union and the Baptist Church. Ralph, like many young men, was impatient and bored, but he would end up being very different than other young men in one important way.

Life had never been easy for Lucetta. She had been married to Niles Crossmire for about thirty years before the trouble really began. Approximately ten years before his death, Niles got himself into financial trouble and put the family farm and a second farm in jeopardy. In order to save the farms, Niles put the properties in Lucetta's name. They had a falling out at the time and Lucetta departed.

Niles eventually got through his financial difficulties and he wanted her to give back the farms. Lucetta nevertheless held onto them, but did not make a living off them. Niles stayed on the family farm until his death a few years later, after which Lucetta moved back to take care of her eighty-three-year-old father-in-law. Lucetta was never a rich woman, but everyone who knew her described her as kind and loving and she had many friends.

The evening of November 19, 1892, was cold and blustery. Lucetta sighed as she donned her coat and stepped outside to do the milking. She stepped into the barn and shut the door behind her. The smell of hay and manure greeted her and she smiled a little. It was a familiar and comforting smell. The cow lowed softly in greeting. She was in need of relief and ready to be milked.

Lucetta lifted her milking stool off the peg and set the bucket under the cow. Suddenly, something behind her made a sound and she felt something slam into her. She twisted, struggling to see her assailant and to get away. In the thin half-light in the barn, she glimpsed her son, Ralph. Her mind struggled to comprehend what was happening. Ralph slapped her, knocking her back into the stall. He wrapped his hands around her throat. Darkness descended as the panic rose. Her lungs burned and she tried to cry out, but there was no air.

Seven-year-old Georgie Herzog stepped into the Crossmire barn to see if Mrs. Lucetta was there. She hadn't answered the door at the house, and his ma had sent him to give her something. For just a second, Georgie glanced around the barn. The cow was standing out of her stall, but Georgie didn't see Mrs. Lucetta there. He saw a large shape hanging from the barn beam farther back, but he could hardly tell what it was. The body swayed and twisted so that suddenly he caught a glimpse of the face. Georgie began screaming and ran for help.

When Sherriff Grubb arrived, he found the neighbors milling around. Their shocked faces said it all. Lucetta Crossmire was hanging from the barn beam, but hanging was not the cause of death. Her face and head were battered. Blood had dried on her face and her hair was matted with blood and gore. Her skirts were ripped off and lay below the body. About four feet away was a scuffed area and puddle of blood that showed where she had fought her attacker. A billet of wood was covered with blood and had been used to crush her skull. If someone had tried to stage the scene so that the police would think she had committed suicide, they did a poor job of it. Everything about the scene bespoke a brutal murder.

Lucetta's only son, Ralph, quickly fell under suspicion. He was not home, and he did not show any shock or upset when confronted with what had happened to his mother. He was the only one who could have gained by her death, and his actions led everyone to believe that he was guilty of the crime. He was quickly arrested. It came out that Ralph had assaulted his mother on previous occasions. He had attempted to buy a life insurance policy on his mother without his mother's knowledge and had threatened her on several occasions. Blood was found on Ralph's clothes when he was arrested and he could not explain it.

During the period before the trial, Ralph fell under suspicion for the murder of his father and the poisoning of a peddler. He would eventually tell a minister that he was "perfectly innocent" of those crimes, but he freely confessed to murdering his mother. Ralph was tried and convicted of the crime. He was sentenced to hang for the murder of his mother and was held at the Smethport Jail.

In December 1893, Ralph Crossmire was hanged. Before the noose was placed around his neck he had something to say. He told the assemblage that if they went through with the hanging him, he would return to haunt the jail. That didn't impress the sheriff or the warden, so they continued with the hanging.

A few days later, an Italian immigrant was arrested and placed in the cell that had recently held Ralph Crossmire. He knew nothing about who had resided in the cell or the threats that Ralph made. Late during his first night in jail, the immigrant began to scream. When the guard answered the call, the immigrant was nearly hysterical. He claimed that a ghost had been in his cell. The spirit of a dark-haired man with a black mustache had leered at him. The immigrant gave a credible description of Ralph Crossmire. Time and again, people placed in the cell where Ralph stayed begged to be let out or to at least change cells. They all told similar stories of a ghastly, ghostly figure and a feeling of personal danger.

Today, the jail is owned by the local historical society and they do allow tours. There is no word on whether Ralph has been seen recently, but the arrogant murderer is very likely still there waiting to terrorize yet another person.

Devil's Run

Trapping was a major occupation on the frontier during the eighteenth century. At Penfield in Elk County there is a tale of three trappers who had an unexpected and unusual experience.

The three trappers were camping outside one night while running trap lines. They were sitting up late by the crackling campfire making plans for the next day when suddenly the flames blazed up. They jumped and saw that beyond the flames there stood a figure silhouetted by the firelight. As the flames died down, the figure stepped forward into the pool of ruddy light. To their horror, they realized that they were entertaining the cloven-hoofed, horned figure of the Devil.

The men turned as one and ran back into the forest, heading for a little settlement that they knew was fifteen miles off. It was a terrible distance, but with the Devil laughing and hot on their heels they had no choice but to flee.

The faster they ran, the more the Devil laughed. He seemed to be putting no effort into the run at all. The men quickly got winded and their breath came in ragged gasps. Stitches tore at their sides and they knew that they couldn't go on. Suddenly, one of the trappers veered to the left off the trail. He crashed through the brush in the darkness, stumbling and falling repeatedly.

In the distance he could hear his friends also crashing in the brush. His mind screamed at him to run. At times he swore that the

Devil was on his heels, and other times he was sure that the Devil had followed his friends and he could rest.

The other two parted as they fumbled through the darkness as well. Each felt that the Devil was following him and that drove them desperately onward.

Two of the men eventually stumbled into the settlement. They were cut up, babbling with terror, and unable to make sense for a time. At last, they poured out their improbable tale. Everyone waited for the third man to arrive. Some people believed the two trappers' story, while others laughed and shook their heads. Imagination got the best of them, some experienced woodsmen muttered, shaking their heads.

The third trapper had not arrived by the next day, and so men from the settlement set out to look for him. Some said that he was in on the prank. Others thought he had fallen and broken "his fool neck." The men hunted all day, but all they found was a barren trail where the vegetation had died. The desolate track was the very trail that the men had run the night before with the Devil on their heels.

In time the trail became known as Devil's Run in remembrance of those men who claimed to have been chased by the Devil along that path. Today the trail has short grass growing on it, but no flowers, trees, or other vegetation. Enlightened people say that the path runs along the length of a glacial deposit and that this has a bearing on why nothing seems to grow there. Perhaps they are right, but then again they are not factoring in another important piece of information. The original inhabitants of the area, the Lenni-Lenape, called that same area "Land of the Devil."

The Disappearance of Doc Haggerty

When oil was found in northern Pennsylvania, a rush began. The oil boom brought roughnecks who were willing to do the dangerous, dirty work of drilling for oil. Among those needed were nitroglycerine shooters, men who could handle the dangerous explosive. Nitroglycerine was notorious for its instability. The explosive liquid could blow up if jostled too much, and that made transporting it a dangerous and often deadly proposition. Nitro-shooters were the men who transported the volatile liquid to the oil drilling sites over rough dirt roads in the back of rattling buckboards in cloth-lined boxes in beds of straw. The nitroglycerine was loaded into "torpedoes" at the well sites and eased down the wells and detonated so that the wells could go deeper and produce more petroleum.

In December 1888, Doc Haggerty was working as a nitro-shooter for the oil wells. He was making a run on what was known locally as the Oil Creek Highway. Oil Creek Highway was a badly rutted dirt road that was notoriously dangerous. Doc Haggerty's load was nearly fourteen hundred pounds of nitroglycerin in felt-lined containers and torpedoes destined for the oil-drilling rigs around Pleasantville. Doc Haggerty was known among the roughnecks as a fearless driver, although some of the men would have also called him foolhardy. He had carefully packed the nitroglycerin in nests of straw and cloth under his seat. His life depended upon how well he had packed the load, so he did the work himself.

Slowly, he started the horses out on the snow-packed, rutted road. He walked the horses along carefully. Beneath him, he could feel the sway and bump of the wagon as it shifted on crude springs. Each bump or dip made him glance back at the load in the wagon. He eased along the road and men at the depot watched him until he disappeared off in the distance. Many of them silently were grateful for the fact that it was Doc Haggerty running that load and not them. As Doc faded into the distance, they turned back to work and thought little about him.

Nearly twenty minutes went by before the terrible explosion broke the silence. The men at the depot instinctively knew what had happened and looked in horror down the road where Doc Haggerty had disappeared. They could see the cloud of dirt and debris in the distance.

The authorities found bits and pieces of the wagon and the horses. Shrapnel-sized hunks of the torpedoes could be located, but there was not one sign of Doc Haggerty. He had simply disappeared from the earth.

Doc Haggerty had taken out a $5,000 insurance policy when he had taken the job as a nitro-shooter. Now his family tried to collect, but the insurance company refused to pay up. They insisted that there was no proof that Doc Haggerty had been blown up in the explosion. He could have jumped off and sent the horses and wagon on to explode, they argued. It could be a case of fraud. Eventually experts were called in to testify, and they stated for the court that the size of the explosion was sufficient to have cremated the body of the unfortunate man.

Nearly a year went by and most of local folks had consigned Doc Haggerty and his death to local folklore. One day in December 1889, a terrible explosion along the Oil Creek Highway ripped through the silence again. Men looked up in horror, wondering who had been blown up now. They hurried down the road, but there was nothing to see. One of the men recollected that it was the anniversary of the death of old Doc Haggerty. The next year the same thing happened on the anniversary of his death. Year after year, people reported hearing a deafening explosion out on the old road.

Doc Haggerty not only relives his death year after year, but also is still seen on occasion, driving his wagon slowly down the road as if he's delivering his full load of nitroglycerin.

Zombie Land

In Mahoning Township, Lawrence County, near the Ohio state line, is a two-acre lot known as Zombie Land. Through the years, this desolate area has been rife with legends, folk stories, and ghostly tales. Zombie Land was the scene of at least one murder and the victim is believed to be one of the many spirits haunting the area.

The little village of Robinson's Corners, near Zombie Land, was once a thriving community along the Mahoning River. There were coal mines and gas wells in the area, the railroad ran nearby, and a trolley operated in the village. It was like hundreds of other little towns in Pennsylvania, but with changing times, the gas wells were no longer lucrative, the coal mines were shut down, and people moved elsewhere. The little village became a ghost town and spirits and stories replaced the people who had once lived there.

One of the oldest tales was of the Light Bulb Heads who once lived along the river near the little town. Legend has it that a group of people suffering from hydrocephalus (water on the brain) moved to the area to live. Because the disease created a deformity, the people were victimized and taunted. Eventually they became reclusive and tried to run off anyone who came near them. Perhaps they were also the origin for another legend about a group of people from a burned-out mental hospital who were said to have settled in the same area. Sadly, they were said to have been harassed and became aggressive with strangers.

The area is riddled with superstitions and legends. A local bridge is known today as the Frankenstein Bridge, or the Puerto Rican Bridge, because of the ethnicity of its early graffiti taggers. According to the blog *Pennsylvania Haunts & History*, there are legends that entities live under the bridge. It is said that if a person's name is spray painted on the bridge, these "bridge people" will kill that person.

Not far from the bridge is an abandoned gas well. Through the years, according to *Pennsylvania Haunts & History*, people have dared each other to light the seeping gas. It is said that the people under the bridge will rise up and attack anyone who disturbs them in such a way.

Nearby there used to be an old residence known as "Blood House." Supposedly, it was the home of a local woman who practiced witchcraft. She was a recluse and shunned the people of the village. On occasion, a child went missing and local folks blamed the old witch for it. She rarely left her home, but on a few occasions she did open the door to chase someone off and curse them. It is believed that if the witch placed a curse on someone, that person would surely die. The house sat abandoned for many years and then burned down mysteriously. There are folks who claim that there are children's graves in the yard.

There are the ruins of the small St. Lawrence Cemetery in the area and stories have long circulated that one of the graves glows at night. Through the years, many young people have visited the cemetery to see the glowing grave. No one in recent years has reported the strange glow, but people still continue to visit in hopes that the grave will glow again.

Zombie Land is also home to a Green Man. There might have been a very prosaic reason for this tale. A local handyman was burned in an electrical fire. He did survive, but the burn scars had a slight greenish tinge. There are people in the area who say they remember the old man working in his garden. It is believed that after his death, he returned to walk the area of Zombie Land near his little house.

The area known today as the "Gravel Road" is actually the railbed for the old Pittsburgh & Lake Erie Railroad (P&LE). People have reported hearing the sound of train whistles there or a roaring wind that rushes over them. Local lore holds that if you park on the current railroad track at night, you will see train lights, hear a train, or "something worse." Of course, "something worse" would eventually happen if you park on train tracks, because a very real train could approach. It is very dangerous to park on railroad tracks and I urge readers not to do it.

Death is a constant theme at Zombie Land. There is an area known as the "Killing Fields," located on each side of East River Road. Local legend says that if you sit there quietly, you will hear gunshots and screams from the long dead.

The most easily verified story of a death in Zombie Land is perhaps the saddest one as well. In 2000, Shannon Leigh Kos was only twelve years old when she was kidnapped by three men who took her to Zombie Land. They raped her and stabbed her to death under the old railroad bridge. They hid her body under Frankenstein Bridge and set it on fire in an attempt to hide the identity. Her body was found partly in Coffee Run. The police determined that Shannon, only in the seventh grade, had been in a relationship with one of her killers, William George Monday, who was twenty-one years old. Monday's two friends and coconspirators were David Christopher Garvey and Perry Sam Ricciardi II, both twenty. This terrible deed has forever colored how people view Zombie Land.

If there is a gentle story associated with this place, it would be the story of the statue of the Virgin Mary. The statue was part of the St. Lawrence Church and Cemetery, located at the site, but is now part of the property of a private residence. The Virgin Mary clasps her hands in prayer as she keeps her eternal vigil; however, it is said that she throws open her arms when it is safe to enter Zombie Land. She is a peaceful presence in a desolate place, but she has not opened her arms in welcome for many years.

Zombie Land was once a lover's lane, a place where teens went to drink and party, and a place where they could frighten each other. There have long been stories of ghostly figures seen walking through the darkness that disappear when approached. The sounds of phantom screams and ghostly voices calling out in the night, and shadowy figures that shift through the darkness around people complete the list of the restless spirits at Zombie Land. Though the walking dead do not shamble through the area, the restless dead do seem to make themselves known there.

Hill View

In 1925, Lawrence County set out to build a facility to house the aged, homeless, and orphaned. They engaged A. L. Thayer to design the facility. At the time there was no centralized facility for the poor in the county. The poor and homeless were "farmed out" to where they could be cared for the cheapest. Many in the county wanted a poor farm, but others wanted a facility that offered services such as medical care.

In 1926, the Lawrence County Home opened its doors. It had a hospital, kitchen, laundry, office space, living quarters for males and females, cemetery, and bomb shelter. The facility was designed as a fully working farm with several outbuildings. Among the first residents were three children.

Only two years after the home opened, there were seventy-two inmates living at the home. During the Great Depression, more and more people arrived.

Newspaper clippings from the *New Castle News* kept by the Lawrence County Historical Society tell the tales of the facility. One headline read, "Inmate of Home Hangs Self to Tree." James Morng, sixty-five years old, was found dead on the ground with a rope around his neck. He had only been at the home for a single day before he committed suicide by hanging himself from a limb of a tree on the grounds. His weight had snapped the limb of the tree and he was found the next morning by another inmate of the home who had gone for a walk.

Another headline from 1929 read, "Despondent Man Slashes Wrist, Is Found Dead." John Knepper, age fifty-eight, was found dead near a stone pile behind the home by a local man. Knepper had slit his left wrist and bled to death; however, the knife was not found at the scene. Despite the missing knife, the coroner ruled the death a suicide.

"Woman Hangs Self To Steam Pipe At Lawrence Co. Home," read yet another headline. Mrs. Schuffert was only forty-four years old when she took an apron and a stocking and made a rope out of them. She hung herself in her room. Her body was found by a matron who brought a breakfast tray to her room.

Eighty-year-old James Wiggins turned up missing for breakfast one morning. The officials at the home found his body on the ground. The headline read, "Fall Fatal to Home Resident." It was believed that Wiggins had climbed out on the roof from the hospital section of the building and fallen off the wall. He was described as "of a wandering disposition" and had previously wandered out in front of a car and been struck.

John Robinson, sixty-four years old, also fell from the building. The headline read, "Home Inmate Is Dead From Fall—Resident At County Home Hurls Self From Window, Dying Of Injuries." According to the home authorities, Robinson's mind had been wandering in recent months. He had removed the screen from his third-floor window and either jumped or fell.

In 1934, sixty-four-year-old Eli Saari and his buddies were drinking late one night on the home property where they also lived. Saari became extremely intoxicated and passed out in a muddy area behind the building. His drinking buddies carried the man to the boiler room in the basement of the facility around 2 A.M. and left him there to sleep it off. Saari died a short while later. His headline read, "Home Inmate Is Found Dead."

Yet another headline: "[Man] Dies Following Drop From Roof." A man, possibly named John Schreider or Mike Wanosk, either jumped or fell from the roof of the county home and died in the hospital hours later. Very little was known about the man except that he had been arrested as a "John Doe" by local police days earlier for acting "queerly," and had subsequently been removed to the county home.

Those are but a few of the many deaths at the Lawrence County Home. Even a doctor committed suicide while working at there. He climbed to the roof and jumped off.

The home typically cared for more than a hundred elderly, and the numbers swelled to nearly two hundred at times, so of course sick and elderly people did die in the building. By 1944, the building became the county nursing home only, having stopped accepting orphans and the poor long before.

In March 1977, the county home completed a new three-story wing. This allowed the facility to accept approximately three dozen more clients. It was at that time that it was decided that the name needed to be changed. Hill View Manor became its official name, but many of the locals would forever call the building either "the poor house" or "the county home."

In 2004, the Hill View Manor was shut down because of financial difficulties. The building needed to be upgraded to meet tightening standards, and the age of the structure made this cost-prohibitive. The building sat empty for several years. It was put up for sale and eventually purchased by Triko Enterprises, but sat unused. Vandals broke in, and by 2007, thieves had stolen the copper wiring, plumbing pipes, and practically anything that was of value.

In 2008, a local resident, Candy Braniff, leased the property because she had heard that it was haunted. She was hoping to ghost hunt there and to offer the site to others who might be interested in doing the same. She has turned Hill View Manor into a business.

Candy has participated in several paranormal television shows that have focused on the site. *Ghost Adventures* was perhaps the most popular show to shoot an episode at Hill View Manor. Zak Bagans and the gang cavorted with spirits and followed Braniff as she gave them a tour of the old nursing home.

Candy has researched the property meticulously, amassing an array of articles about the facility. She gathered every document she could find about the deaths at the home, and she even identified all who were laid to rest in the cemetery behind the main building. Her research continued as she connected with former employees of the facility who helped her pin down exactly who some of the spirits are. She also had psychics visit the property to help her locate the most haunted areas.

The resident ghosts include a little boy named Jeffrey, who was among the first residents of the facility when it was a poor house. Jeffrey first made himself known while the facility was still open. According to former staff, an elderly patient on the second floor one day rang for the nurse. She asked the nurse to do something about the little boy in her room who said he was cold. She described the child and said that he was wearing a sweater but was unable get warm. No one else could see the "child" and they assumed that the elderly lady was hallucinating.

Several years later, however, another elderly woman in the same room rang for a nurse. She insisted that there was a little boy in her room who was very cold. She was distressed and wanted to have the nurse help the child. She insisted that his little sweater was not keeping him warm. The story got around and the nurse who had heard the story years earlier was shocked to hear that the second woman had described the same child—right down to the sweater. Candy Braniff, the only other person who knew the story, hired a psychic, who sensed the child. The boy has also been said to communicate with ghost hunters who visit the site.

Another popular spirit is Mary Virginia. She was an elderly little lady who died in the facility. She loved shiny watches and bracelets and little baubles. When a psychic described Mary Virginia to Candy, she immediately knew who she was. She had spoken to former employees who remembered dear little Mary Virginia. People often bring Mary Virginia little shiny gifts when they ghost hunt there. Mary Virginia has been recorded talking to ghost hunters and others have seen baubles move.

The third floor is popular because black shadows flit along the hallways and along the nursing station. They have been both seen with the naked eye and recorded on tape. What makes the third floor so popular is the fact that the black shadowy figures seem to move along all the time.

The police through the years have been called to the property because of vandalism and thrill seekers. Some of the officers freely talk about having to enter the building when it was abandoned. They have seen figures looking out the windows once they had secured the building and knew that no one was inside. They have heard footsteps follow them even when they could clearly see that no one was physically there.

There is a large black mass said to haunt the hallway to the basement, and it has been seen walking the hall and going down into the basement.

The piano in the cafeteria is known to play on its own, but it is not the only strange phenomenon a person could experience there. Peggy Julian, a former cook at Hill View Manor, told *Ghost*

Adventurers that while she was working one evening, she had an encounter. The lights turned off on their own and the double doors swung open by themselves. Peggy froze and waited. A few minutes later the lights came back on and the doors closed by themselves as well.

In the new section of the building, there is the story of Amanda. Amanda was an elderly patient at the nursing home who was wheelchair bound. She loved to feed the birds and each morning she wheeled herself outside to do so. One morning she got confused, and instead of going back into the main hall she made a wrong turn and fell down the stairs into the basement. She died there. She has been felt and heard in that hallway. Jim is another spirit at the former nursing home. He often speaks on tape to the people who come to ghost hunt.

The cemetery has its own stories to tell. In 1971, human bone fragments turned up in the backyard of Hill View Manor. According to county records that Candy Braniff uncovered, part of the neighboring golf course sits on cemetery ground. Furthermore, records indicate that some graves might have more than one person buried in them. There are ghostly encounters associated with the cemetery plot.

When Hill View Manor shut down, the records and personal possessions of many of the residents and former residents were left behind. Some of those belongings are believed to have spirits associated with them.

The chapel is considered to be haunted as well. People report being touched, hearing voices, and seeing figures inside. The chapel doors have reputedly opened by themselves many times.

In 2011 a film student, Noel, filmed a short documentary at Hill View Manor at night. The production assistant and Noel were talking over the radio when a disembodied voice interfered in their conversation and spoke about what they were doing. Many paranormal groups visit the building for a night and walk away with physical evidence such as orbs, EVP, and strange anomalies in photos and videos. Others talk of being touched, pushed, pinched, or grabbed, or report objects moving, doors opening, and disembodied voices.

Murder Swamp

New Castle in Lawrence County is only a stone's throw from the Ohio border. It is a town filled with hard-working people of diverse, ethnic backgrounds, where the financial times are evident in the empty buildings and "For Sale" signs. On the edge of New Castle is a place that is nearly forgotten today, but it was once a deadly place—Murder Swamp.

Murder Swamp is a marshy area of the Beaver River. Its history dates back to the mid-1920s, when the Cleveland mafia used the area as a dump site for bodies.

Murder Swamp came to the public's attention when it again became a dump site for bodies, this time for a serial killer who stalked Cleveland and western Pennsylvania. It all began in September 1943, when the torso of a woman's body washed up on the shore of Lake Erie, near Cleveland. The police could not identify the body. In the following year, in a rough area known as Kingsbury Run, two male corpses were found. Their bodies were mutilated and they had been beheaded. Before they had been dumped, their genitals had been removed. The younger of the two victims was a small-time crook; the other man was unidentified. The next year, two more bodies were found in Kingsbury Run. A prostitute was found cut up in a basket near a butcher shop and a man was decapitated. Now the press realized that they had a serial killer on the loose. The *Cleveland Plain Dealer* labeled the killer "the Mad Butcher of Kingsbury Run."

Two more corpses were found mutilated and the Mad Butcher had a death toll of at least seven dead. In an amazing twist, Elliot Ness of *The Untouchables* fame had taken a job as the director of safety for Cleveland and assigned several detectives to the case. One of the detectives, Peter Merlyo, began to look at past murders in the area. He discovered that in the 1920s, several bodies had been found in an area of Pennsylvania near New Castle. Because of the number of bodies found there, the locals had nicknamed the area Murder Swamp. Three headless bodies had been found in Murder Swamp in 1925. The area was remote and people believed that it was used because it was a convenient area in which to dispose of bodies. Now, Detective Merlyo reevaluated the murders. The similarities between the 1925 murders and those in Kingsbury Run were striking.

The first body from 1925 was a young man who was found naked on October 6. The medical examiner stated that the body had been dead for approximately three weeks. The man had been decapitated and could not be identified. Two days later the man's head was located in the swamp, but still authorities were unable to identify the victim.

A second headless male skeleton was found on October 17, 1925, in the swamp. The man's skull was found two days later. On that same day another skull was found. The last skull was that of a woman whom the medical examiner estimated had been dead for approximately one year. Her torso was never found.

Ness and his force continued to find bodies in Pittsburgh, near New Castle, and in Kingsbury Run. In total, five bodies were found in Murder Swamp. Several of the victims were hobos or prostitutes, and this led the police to think that the murderer was either homeless or was moving through that community. They rousted large shantytowns, burned them down, and arrested many of the vagrants while looking for clues to the identity of the serial killer. They postulated that the killer rode the rails or had a route of some sort that he traveled from New Castle through Cleveland and back again. Bodies found along that route bolstered the idea. They all followed the modus operandi for the serial killer: decapitation, mutilation, removal of the genitals, and often severed the limbs.

There were always more questions than answers in the case of the Mad Butcher killings. The bodies were not killed where they were found. Did the Mad Butcher have a lair where he could do his foul deeds in private? Some of the victims had been decapitated while alive, and that also seemed to indicate that the murderer had a secure place to torture and kill them. The skill used to sever the bodies and remove the genitals led the police to think that this murderer had some medical training. It seemed obvious that he had more than a passing knowledge of human anatomy.

Eventually, the police narrowed down the suspects to Dr. Frank Sweeney. Sweeney was from Kingsbury Run, was large and powerful, had a violent streak, was a known alcoholic, and was rumored to be bisexual; however, he was not an easy suspect. His cousin was Senator Martin L. Sweeney, and so inquiries had to be made discretely.

Sweeney was far from a broken derelict. He was a smart, quick-witted man who seemed to enjoy locking wits with Ness and his detectives. Sweeney's story is shrouded in mystery. In August 1938, he was interrogated by Elliot Ness and his team. Sweeney was held in a local hotel for several days during the questioning. Ness brought in one of the inventors of the lie detector test and had it administered repeatedly. The consensus was that Sweeney was lying.

After he was released, Sweeney had himself committed to a psychiatric facility. He would voluntarily spend the rest of his life in a series of such facilities; however, from time to time he would check himself out. Officially, the series of murders labeled as the work of the Mad Butcher ended as well. Unofficially, similar murders continued to happen both in the Pittsburgh and Cleveland area as well as elsewhere.

Another suspect was Frank Dolezal who was an alcoholic from the Kingsbury Run area and had frequented the same bar as some of the known victims. Dolezal was fingered by a private detective hired to look into the crime and possibly to clear the name of Frank Sweeney. No one has ever definitively solved the case, and so it is still a matter of discussion today.

As for those possible first victims found in Murder Swamp, they have been all but forgotten in the mists of time. Perhaps that is why they are said to haunt Murder Swamp. Each of the five victims discarded there have been rumored to appear on occasion to those unlucky enough to wander into the area where their earthly remains were scattered. People have claimed to see figures walking along that disappear if approached.

Others say that the Mad Butcher himself haunts this first killing field. No matter who the Mad Butcher really was, he is most assuredly dead by now. Is his spirit wandering his first dump site, and if so why? Is he revisiting his crime scenes? Or is he filled with remorse and horror as he faces the specters of those whom he so callously killed long ago?

Phantoms, ghostly voices, and strange darting lights are reported at Murder Swamp. Perhaps the spirits there are trying to tell us of their demise or even where they are buried.

On the Beaver River there are little unnamed islands just off Murder Swamp. In 1952, two men were exploring one of those islands when they unearthed an old, shallow sandy grave. In it were the skeletal remains of a forty-year-old woman who had been strangled by her own belt months earlier. She could not be a victim of the Mad Butcher, but it would surprise no one if her restless spirit has added to the denizens of the dead who haunt Murder Swamp.

The Laurel Highlands

THE LAUREL HIGHLANDS AWED THE FIRST WHITE MEN WHO CLIMBED THE mountains there. It is a region where only the strong could survive. The French and Indian War raged through the area, and the settlers had to fight for their very lives. But in the Laurel Highlands, people had to fight not only other men, but also the elements. The ghosts of this region range from those at the world-famous Bedford Springs Hotel to the strange story of the Dick family.

Old Bedford Village and so many other sites offer ghostly tales that illustrate what life in the Laurel Highlands is all about. Read on and enter the world of forts, phantoms, and haunted history.

Polly Williams's Tragic Death

In 1808, Polly Williams was a pretty sixteen-year-old girl with blonde hair who had taken a job with the Jacob Moss family. She caught the eye of a local young man, Philip Rodgers, who was twenty-three years old. He came from a good family and was well regarded in the area.

Philip began to court Polly and they grew very close. Soon, he asked her to marry him and they became betrothed. Polly's family had moved westward two years earlier, so she had no family in the area to watch over her. The Moss family treated her as a ward, however, and kept a close eye on her.

Mr. and Mrs. Moss spoke to Polly about when she and young Rodgers were planning to wed. Polly had hoped it would be soon, but when she pressed Philip, he insisted that they wait two years.

On occasion, Polly asked Philip about shortening the engagement, but he would grow violently angry. They argued about the wedding date, and his anger and cruelty made her cry.

One night, Polly returned to the Moss home crying. Mrs. Moss pressed her about what had happened. Tearfully, Polly told her employer about the fighting and Philip's hateful anger. She confided that there were times when she was afraid for her life. She believed that Philip was capable of murder.

Mrs. Moss counseled the girl to break her engagement, but Polly felt bound by the arrangement. No one else had shown interest in her for some time, because of Philip's explosive anger, and she did not want to die an old maid. She wept and told Mrs. Moss that she desperately loved Philip.

On August 17, 1810, Philip finally seemed ready to wed Polly. He told her that he had arranged for a squire from Chestnut Ridge to marry them. Philip asked Polly to meet him at their favorite spot on Laurel Mountain, the cliff known as White Rocks, above their hometown of Fairechance.

On that morning, Polly put on her best dress and set off for the mountain to meet Philip. She did not return that night, but because she had dropped hints that she and Philip might wed, people were not unduly worried by her absence.

The next day, some children picking berries up on the mountain found Polly's battered body at the foot of White Rocks. At first it was supposed that she had jumped or been pushed. However, the coroner, Thomas Collins, stated at the inquest that Polly had been bludgeoned by a sharp rock, which had left several wounds "in and upon the back of the head and side of the face . . . giving her several mortal wounds of the length of three inches, and of the depth of one inch," according to an 1871 article in the Uniontown newspaper *Genius of Liberty*. Her body had been dumped under the cover of the rocks at the foot of the cliff after her murder.

Philip Rodgers was arrested for the crime and he went to trial. He was found not guilty because of a lack of evidence. It was speculated at the time that Rodgers struck down Polly because she told him that she was with child. No one ever publically confirmed or denied that story, but it was the only possible logical motive for the violent crime. Rodgers had no alibi for the time in question, but since no motive was found, the jury could not find him guilty. Rodgers went free and Polly was buried only two miles from where she died. Her tombstone reads: "Polly Williams, who was found murdered by her seducer at The White Rocks, August 17, 1810, AGED, 18 YEARS." It seemed that public opinion had found Rodgers guilty of the crime despite his legal acquittal.

There are many versions of the story that are more or less dramatic than the one told here. In one version, Rodgers returned years later to White Rocks and jumped off, but there is no documentation for that event. Many stories were told, but the main facts are true: Pretty Polly Williams was murdered at White Rocks. Perhaps that is why Polly is said to still haunt the area. People claim to see the young girl walking through the mists early in the morning, as if waiting impatiently for the man who would take her life. Perhaps she prefers to return and dream of her marriage, children, and the life she was denied. It would be a bitter pill for poor Polly to accept that her lover played her false and took her life. Her ghost is said to smile softly and fade away when she realizes that she is being observed.

Fallingwater

Frank Lloyd Wright was famous for his unique architectural style. He believed that a building should blend into nature and become part of the peaceful scene. The clean and revolutionary designs won him accolades and made him a very sought-after architect and furniture designer. One of Wright's crowning jewels was a home he designed in 1935 in western Pennsylvania that he named Fallingwater. The home was built at Bear Run Waterfall and Wright used the elements of nature to inspire the home. In 1991, Fallingwater was named as the "best all-time work of American architecture" by the American Institute of Architects.

The house was commissioned by Edgar J. Kaufmann, owner of the Kaufmann's department store chain, and it served as his family's summer home from 1937 to 1963.

The master bedroom at Fallingwater is said to be haunted by a woman in a white nightgown. She is seen gazing sadly at the waterfalls. The story of how she came to haunt the lovely home is a sad and all too common tale.

The woman is believed to be Liliane Kaufmann, Edgar's wife. Edgar was a serial cheater, and Liliane had to live through the disgrace of his many lovers; however, Edgar always returned to Liliane after a fling—that was, until the last affair.

As Liliane's health was failing, she came to learn that Edgar was having yet another affair. This one, however, would end differently than all the others. Edgar supposedly confronted Liliane and demanded a divorce. He wanted to marry his new paramour. Liliane contested the divorce, because she loved her husband and also because Edgar was holding her to a prenuptial agreement that left her penniless. In the end, Edgar won and Liliane died.

Liliane was buried in Homewood Cemetery, not far away. After Edgar's death, Liliane's body was exhumed and moved back to Fallingwater. Sculptor Alberto Giacometti was commissioned by Liliane and Edgar's son to create the great bronze doors of her crypt. Their son placed both his parents in the crypt so that even if they could not be together in life, they would be together in death. The bronze doors are hauntingly reminiscent of the lives of the two. A woman sitting against a tree is etched on one panel, while the man stands in the distance as a storm brews in the scene. Some security guards at the site have reported seeing a woman in a white nightgown gazing forlornly at the falls. Could it really be Liliane reflecting upon her broken life and marriage in the home she and Edgar once shared?

The Haunted Bedford Springs

The Bedford Springs Hotel is a grand building sitting just a mile outside of the town it is named after. On the grounds of the hotel are seven springs with waters containing minerals, long thought to have medicinal value. Before the first white men ever set foot in

Bedford County, the native people made pilgrimages there to ingest and bathe in the mineral waters. Different springs held reputedly different medicinal values.

There are three different versions of how the springs came to the attention of British settlers. The oldest version dates to 1796. In this version, a man by the name of Nicholas Stouffler discovered the mineral springs while searching for gold in the area. Stouffler became convinced that he had found something of great value. A local history described Stouffler as a "queer sort of man."

In the second version, dating to 1804, James Fletcher, a local businessman who had suffered for years from rheumatism and sores on his legs, went fishing and discovered the springs. He partook of the waters, and later that night his pain eased; he slept better than he had in years. Fletcher made a connection between having taken the waters and his improving health. The next day, he returned to drink more water and bathe his legs as well. Within weeks, Fletcher found that the ulcers had healed and the rheumatism had abated. He told others who were suffering about the healing waters in the springs above town and they, too, sought relief there. By the following year, people were coming in carriages and wagons. Those who were ill journeyed many days on the strength of the testimonials they had heard about the healing powers of the waters in the springs above Bedford.

In yet a third version, the honor of discovering the springs was given to Dr. George D. Foulke, who practiced medicine for some time in Bedford County. During those years he struck up a friendship with Dr. George Anderson, and the two young men made the discovery of the springs during a hunting trip. They recognized the medicinal value of the waters and returned home to tell Dr. John Anderson, George's father, about it. John Anderson realized the value of such medicinal springs and saw a business opportunity. At that time in Europe, "taking the waters" had become the rage. Well-to-do Europeans who were immigrating to America were looking for places where they could continue the practice of bathing in or drinking medicinal waters. In 1798, John Anderson was able to buy that parcel of land and began to deepen the springs by digging them out. He also improved the land and made it more accessible to people.

The land where the springs are had already seen service as the site of the Caledonia Iron Works, which sat near what is today known as the Black Spring. An inn was also built to house the many people who were already visiting the springs. John Anderson built a house on the property. There he treated, and even housed, many of the people visiting the springs. He probably prescribed the waters of the springs to his patients.

Visitors also lived in tents or wagons while their loved ones took the healing waters. In 1806, Anderson built the Stone Inn from locally quarried stone. The inn was not large enough to house all who came to take the waters. He continuously added on to the hotel through the years, until the buildings stretched out to nearly one fifth of a mile. The completed hotel had 453 rooms.

The hotel's waters brought many visitors to the hotel. It was not long before the wealthy and famous began to arrive for the benefits the springs offered. The hotel slowly changed from a mecca for the ill to a fashionable resort for the wealthy.

One early visitor was former vice president Aaron Burr. In 1806, he arrived at Bedford Springs with his daughter, Theodosia Burr Alston, and her small son, Aaron Burr Alston. Theodosia was a remarkable woman who was well educated and articulate. She had often sought out mineral waters for herself, but when her small son became ill, she decided to take him to Bedford Springs. Records indicate that young Aaron failed to regain his health while at the springs, and he died in 1812.

Ten presidents visited the Bedford Springs Hotel, seven of whom were in office at the time. In 1848, James K. Polk was the first sitting president to come to the hotel. Pennsylvania president James Buchanan first stayed at the hotel before his term. He frequented the Bachelor's Quarters, also known as the Crockford, throughout his many stays there. During Buchanan's administration (1857–1861), the Bedford Springs became known as "the summer White House," in reference to his long summer stays. The first transatlantic telegram was delivered to Buchanan at the hotel from Queen Victoria. In all, Buchanan spent forty summers at the hotel.

The Bedford Springs Hotel also built the first indoor Olympic-sized swimming pool. The hotel added an outdoor swimming pool, tennis courts, and other recreational areas through the years. The golf course in particular has long been popular.

During World War II, from 1941 to 1943, the hotel was pressed into service to house a radio operator school for the Navy. In 1943, it became a prisoner-of-war camp for Japanese diplomats captured during the war. The building served this purpose through 1945.

During the early 1980s, the hotel fell on hard times. The public was no longer interested in a posh hotel, and the doors eventually shut. It looked like the days of luxury and joy for the Bedford Springs were over, but in 2004, restoration work began on the hotel. It took $120 million, but the hotel is once again a world-class facility. It has the charm of yesteryear and today's conveniences. With a spa, hiking trails, nearby lake, and famous golf course, it is once again a glittering jewel in the heart of the Allegheny Mountains.

Many of the ghost stories about the Bedford Springs Hotel revolve around people who lived or worked there. One of the most popular is about a Japanese diplomat who was interned at the hotel during World War II. According to local lore, the diplomat was an older gentleman who dressed daily in his uniform and decked his chest with all of his medals. He was not allowed to wander the grounds, so he paced or marched up and down the screened-in porch. He was chafing at being held as a prisoner of war, not able to serve his nation. As the story goes, he died of a heart attack one day in his room. Shortly after his death, people began to say that they saw the ghost of the diplomat walking the sun porch. Official records indicate that the only Japanese prisoner of war to die at the Bedford Springs Hotel was a Japanese cook. Was the diplomat's death omitted from the public record because in a time of war a diplomat's death could have caused international scandal? Or had people somehow confused the story?

In that same hall, a couple years ago, a friend of one of the current staff photographed the image of a young woman in a long dress in the hallway where the diplomat was said to walk. The identity of the young woman is unknown. Guests and staff have mentioned seeing a young girl, about seven or eight, on the first floor. She seems to be happy, and she appears for a moment before passing on.

Two ghosts have been reported in the swimming pool area. One is of a young child named "Hannah" or "Anna." Her voice was caught as EVP by a paranormal investigator (www.ghostsrus.com). The child is seen along the pool, but never in it. There is no record of a child drowning in the pool, but children have died on the property through the years.

At the near end of the pool area are two staircases where musicians once played for the amusement of the swimming patrons. In that area, an elderly woman has been seen. She is solidly built and wears a blue dress that dates her to the 1940s or 1950s. She seems to appear and watch at the pool before fading away.

During the years when the hotel was not open, security guards walked the hotel each night in order to keep out trespassers. Those guards have their own stories to tell. In 2002, I had the opportunity to interview several guards from the Bedford Springs Hotel before it was renovated. Nearly every guard admitted to hearing footsteps and voices speaking down empty corridors, and to seeing shadows slinking along the walls as they did their tours of the building. Most of them said that when they were not doing a walkthrough, they preferred to stay in the guard shack, which was located in the built-in sun porch.

One man said that he had not personally ever had an experience in the building, but his wife had. About 11:30 P.M. one night, the guard's wife brought him his supper because he had forgotten to take his packed lunch earlier. The guard left the door to the sun porch open for her to enter in case she got there while he was still doing his walkthrough. She came inside and heard what sounded like a party going on in the darkened main entry hall. As she could clearly see that the entry hall was dark, she assumed that what she was hearing was a radio playing in the entry hall area. The sounds of music, talking, and clinking glasses made her think that her husband was listening to some sort of radio show.

The guard's wife sat on a chair just outside the shack and waited for her husband. As she listened, she realized that whatever was going on was not a show because there was no narration and she could not understand what any of the voices were saying. It was as though they were talking just softly enough that she could hear the words but not quite make them out. She walked over to the darkened entry hall a few times, but the sounds did not get louder when she got closer. She began to feel uneasy and a chill ran up her spine. What was her husband listening to, she wondered?

She heard footsteps approaching and turned to see her husband's flashlight bobbing through the darkness toward the lit guard shack area. Just as her husband stepped into the pool of light where the guard shack sat, the sound of voices and music stopped as if someone had turned off the radio. She explained what she heard to her husband and asked him what he had been listening to. Her husband insisted that he had not had the radio on. He pointed to the guard shack and she could clearly see the radio on the desk.

"Then there's somebody in there," she said, pointing toward the darkened entry hall.

"That's impossible," he said. He walked over to the entrance to the entry hall and clicked on his powerful flashlight. "Come look at this," he instructed her.

Reluctantly, she got up and walked over. Instinctively, she knew she was not going to like what she saw. The light showed a drop off of about four feet down to the dirt floor. Someone had pried up all of the boards that would have created the floor to the entry hall. All that was left were roughhewn beams with planks laid across them to make a bridge to the back of the entry hall. There was no place for a person to walk and no way that a group of people could have been in that area. She watched her husband's light play along the walls and realized that there was no place for a radio to sit either. Without a further word, she dropped the subject but also told her husband that she would not be delivering dinner anymore.

Another security guard spoke about a woman he had repeatedly encountered on the second floor. She was a young lady with her hair pulled back in a bun and she wore a gray skirt and white blouse. On her head was an old-fashioned cap, like a nurse's cap, but with scallops across the top of it. The woman seemed aware that the guard was watching her and turned to hurry away. On different occasions he chased her down the second- or third-floor hallways until she disappeared into a room. He was not sure how she did it, but he was very sure that this young woman was a trespasser who was managing to give him the slip.

One night, the security guard encountered her yet again on his walkthrough. She was on the second-floor hallway between him and the one staircase. He was sure that now he had her, because the staircase behind her was walled up at the bottom end, and there was nowhere else for her to go this time. He called out to get her attention and she paused for a moment as if startled. Suddenly, she turned and ran toward the closed-off staircase. She rushed into the darkness and down the stairs; the guard was only steps behind her. He was sure that this time he was going to catch the woman. He rushed downstairs and smacked into the plywood barrier at the bottom. The security guard flashed his light around, but there was no one there.

The guard refused to even think the word "ghost." He continued to encounter the woman, but he no longer pursued her. After all, the owners wanted the property protected from vandals and that woman was certainly not a vandal.

Yet another guard talked about a misty form that he encountered on numerous occasions in the old servant's hallway. He would see a white misty shape taking form. He never stayed around long enough to find out if it was male or female, but he was certain that it was taking a human shape.

During the restoration, some of the construction workers, artisans, carpet layers, and electricians had their own experiences. They talked about phantom footsteps passing them, tools that disappeared and reappeared, the feeling of being touched when no one was there, and other ghostly manifestations. Some of the men even talked about hearing their names called out.

Other staff members at the hotel have also reported strange experiences. One of the night watchmen told his superiors that he has seen a little girl in a period dress near the area where elevator #3 now stands. The child merely appears and then fades away.

One of the staff reportedly was in the swimming pool area with her brother taking photos during the Christmas season. Suddenly, they both felt something run between them "like a gust of wind." They froze, looking at each other, and then heard a child laughing softly in the direction in which the wind had gone.

A male staff member was tidying up some towels one night when he felt something brush past him. The towel on a nearby

chair shifted and fell to the floor as if it had been bumped by someone, but he saw no one. The only people there were in the pool.

A former maid contacted me about her experiences in the hotel. She said that she and other maids consistently encountered a playful spirit in one of the rooms on the second floor. Each maid was carefully instructed on how to clean and dress out the room for the coming guests. There was a small welcome card that was to be sitting on the dresser so that it was the first thing the guests saw when entering the room. On several occasions, the girls had gotten in trouble for not having the signs in the right place. The maids all insisted that they had put the cards where they were supposed to be. One day, a young maid finished a room and stood in the doorway to check it one more time. Somehow the card was turned away from the doorway. Exasperated, she stomped back into the room and turned the card back. "Now leave it alone or you'll get me fired," she barked at the room at large. Suddenly, the card flew off the dresser and across the room. It was as if someone did not like being spoken to that way and had slapped the card off the dresser. The maid froze for a second, and then walked across the room and picked up the card. She laid it back on the dresser. "I'm serious, you'll get me fired. Please stop it." She talked more softly this time and the card remained at rest. The young woman had long suspected that the room was haunted and now she knew that it was. Other young maids also had the same problem. The young women were convinced that a spirit was in that room.

According to another staff member, an employee had an experience in the spa section of the hotel. The spa is built in the area where an older structure once stood. One night, one of the supervisors had walked into one of the rooms in the spa section. As she stood there, the figure of an older woman in Victorian clothing suddenly materialized, sitting on an ottoman. The supervisor froze, watching the woman for a few seconds before she faded away. A few weeks later she was looking through some old photographs with her family and she froze. There was a picture of the Victorian woman she had seen in the room at the Bedford Springs Hotel. The woman was a past relative of the supervisor. Why she had come to the hotel and materialized is still unknown.

In 2004, the Ghost Research Foundation spent two nights in the old hotel and they took thousands of photographs in the building;

however, the most definitive evidence was EVP they caught in the building. On the third-floor level above the central part of the building an investigator captured the sound of a horse and carriage pulling up to the building. In the swimming pool, the sound of a little girl giving her name was also heard.

Bedford Tavern

The Bedford Tavern sits on land deeded from the Penn family to Jacob Wikoff in 1802. In 1839, the property was sold to Alice Fyan, who also bought an adjoining property. The Fyan family owned the property for approximately a hundred years; therefore, the history of the house parallels the history of the Fyan family. Robert Fyan Jr., Alice's husband, had been in the hotel industry and also owned a general store in Cambria County. He moved the family to Bedford in 1836 and opened his store there three years later. Alice bought the property approximately one year before her husband's death in 1870. After Robert died, his son William took over the business. In 1940, the Fyan family sold the business to the Gephart family. They opened the Gephart Inn, a restaurant and hotel. The family only ran the establishment for six years but the next owners, the Stayer Family, maintained the name for the establishment. Eventually the Stayer family opened a bar and lounge in the basement of the building. In 1949, the Stayers also changed the name of the establishment to the Bedford Hotel.

In 1981, the May family took over and earned the hotel a reputation for good food, especially seafood. In 2006, Jeff Rinscheid and B. J. Taylor purchased the building. They have continued to improve the hotel through remodeling, fine dining, and a friendly atmosphere. The food earned the hotel a column in the *New York Times* food section. The hotel, however, has another claim to fame—it is haunted. In fact, it is so haunted that it was featured in the October 2012 premiere episode of *My Ghost Story* on the Biography Channel.

Long before the current owners took over, the hotel had a reputation for hauntings. Perhaps one of the most common spirits is that of a man many of the staff have seen coming down the back stairs from the first floor to the basement bar level. When he comes down, he heads for the bar. Other staff members say they have seen a man sitting at the bar who disappears when they turn to serve him.

Another ghost reported is a traveling salesman. People have been able to rent rooms by the month at the tavern, and this salesman had done so during the 1990s. He was often gone for days at a time, so no one was worried when he had not been seen for a few days. One night, however, a patron came in and mentioned that the salesman's car was parked by the laundromat behind the hotel. The owner confirmed that it was the salesman's car and went to the salesman's room. He knocked on the door but there was no answer. There was, however, a terrible smell that confirmed his worst fears. The owner called the police and they went in. The poor man had died from a heart attack and had been lying for several days in his bed. After the tragic death, the owners decided to redo the room. They had gotten rid of the mattress immediately, but now they decided to also put a new bed frame in the room. They took the old frame upstairs for storage and assembled a new bed. That night, terrible pounding came from the room. It sounded like someone was pounding on the walls. The owners were called and they went in. They found the bed shoved against the wall. The nightly pounding continued until they put the old bed frame back in the room.

On the first floor below the room where the salesman died, the tenants began to experience doors opening and closing by themselves. As they were running a business from the rooms, they decided to replace the doors with curtains because curtains ruffling upset the patrons less. You could blame that on the wind.

At the stop of the stairs from the bar are the main bathrooms. Each night the bar manager locked up the bar, went up those stairs, and finished locking up. She exited the building through the door just opposite the bathrooms. As she prepared to step out at 2 A.M. one night, the men's room commode flushed. Shocked, the bar manager hurried back in. She had nearly locked a bar patron in. She swore that there was no one in the building, but someone had to be there. She stepped in and knocked on the door. There was not a sound, so she opened the men's room door. No one was there. She shut it and prepared to step out again. Once more, the commode flushed. Her mind grasped for rational answers. Someone had to have been hiding behind the bathroom door. She hadn't looked there. This time she threw open the door and peered gingerly behind it. No one was there. Again she shut the door and opened the outside door. Once more the commode flushed behind her. She froze for a second. "Whoever you are," she muttered, "have a good time. Good night." She stepped out and firmly locked the door. No one living was in the building.

On the basement bar floor there are many odd things that happen. On several occasions the soda tap that sits in a holder has risen up like a cobra and turned itself around before being dropped. No one is ever near it when this happens, but bar patrons and staff alike have witnessed this happening.

There is a row of fish tanks along the one back wall on the bar level. A dart board is on the back wall and behind it is the door that goes into the area where you can access the fish tanks. The dart board weighs about seventy pounds, and is not something that is easy to move. One afternoon, owner Jeff Rinscheid came in and found the dart board pulled away and the door to the back area open. Jeff called out to make sure no one was back there, and then closed the door and pushed the dart board back in place. When his bar manager came out of the kitchen, he asked her why the door had been left open. She stopped short. "Open? It can't be. When I came in at 4:45 P.M., I found it open, closed it, and then moved the dart board back in front of the door." No one else was there, so who kept opening the door?

One afternoon, two residents were talking to Jeff at the bar while having dinner. They were the only three people in the building at the time. Suddenly, Jeff heard a song whistled behind his left shoulder. The notes were repeated three times. Jeff turned to see who had come in, but no one was there. He turned to the diners and asked if they had heard anything. The look on the one man's face was answer enough. The guy nodded. "I heard whistling. Yes."

One Monday afternoon, when the building was closed, Jeff was working in his office. He heard a woman call out "Jeff" clearly. Not thinking anything of it, Jeff got up to see who was there. No one was in the room, in the hall, or even on the stoop outside. The front door was locked. Shaking his head, Jeff went back to work. Since that time, he has heard his name called many times. Some of the staff members have also heard their names called, too.

People report shadows moving along, glimpses of a man who looks very much like the owner and is seen in the building when he is not there, and hearing ghostly voices. Sometimes they hear two women talking, but no one can make out quite what they are saying. The area of the men's room is often very active. Some people even feel watched in that room. Jeff's attitude toward the haunting is to take it all in stride. He looks upon it as an adventure, and truly it is.

Jean Bonnet Tavern

The Jean Bonnet Tavern was built by Robert Callender on land he acquired in 1762. Some historic records for the county from 1719 list an old abandoned French fort at the junction of two Indian trails and then offer an estimate of how many miles it would be from Fort Bedford to the crossroads. By looking at a map from that time, it is easy to see that the two Indian trails are now Routes 30 and 31, so the old abandoned French fort could possibly be the first floor of the Jean Bonnet. If this is so, Callender would have only built the upper floors. Callender was a British trader and businessman, and he opened the building as a tavern and inn.

According to legend, Callender brought a beautiful young woman with him to run the tavern and inn. The young woman had a vested interest in making sure that the business was successful, because she was not only Callender's employee—she was also his mistress. The young woman's name has been lost through time, but her story remains.

It is said that the young woman believed that Callender was going to marry her someday. She felt guilty about her "sinful" life as his mistress. She occasionally tried to encourage him to marry her. At those times, Callender would suddenly have to leave on business. In truth, Callender could not marry the young woman because he already had a wife and children in Greensburg; however, the young woman did not know about Callender's family, and so she kept hoping and dreaming about her life as his wife.

Once when Callender was away on business, the young woman fell ill. She grew more ill by the day and suddenly it seemed imperative for her to straighten things out with God before she died. She sent word to Callender that she was dying and begged him to come back to marry her. She waited as the days slipped by. Each time she heard a horse riding into the yard, she would rise up and look to see if it was Robert. In the last days she could no longer rise, but she still believed that Robert would soon be by her side and ready to marry her. She died still believing and hoping.

Accounts of the young woman haunting the building have long existed. Stories in the newspaper date back many years. People have reported feeling someone rushing past them on the second and third floors. Others have heard the rustle of skirts and some have felt the young woman's anxiousness and pain. Few, however, have seen her.

Several years ago, a retired brigadier general contacted me with an extraordinary tale. He explained that one cold winter's evening he and his wife were driving back to Pittsburgh on the turnpike when they decided to get off at the Bedford exit and take a break by stopping at the Jean Bonnet Tavern. They had passed it many times, but had never taken the opportunity to visit it until that night.

They pulled into the parking lot and were surprised to see that the building was all but empty. They entered the second-floor bar area and found that although it was only about 8 P.M. the staff was closing down. Apparently the cold had convinced folks to stay home, so the bartender was closing up. The bartender and waitresses were cordial to the couple and got them some hot coffee to go. They apologized for the inconvenience and graciously asked the couple if they wanted to walk through the building. The general and his wife thanked them and said that they would return another time. The bartender asked them if they minded going down the stairs to the first floor and out that way. She had just mopped the bar floor and it would be safer if they went down through the first floor.

The couple went down the stairs. The first floor was dark other than the emergency exit lights. The general's wife saw a lit sign for the restrooms and asked him to wait a moment so that she could use the facilities.

While his wife was in the restroom, the general looked around at the room. He turned to glance to his right and suddenly found himself looking at an amazing sight. He saw a petite young woman with long blond hair staring at him. She was hovering about four inches above the floor and he could not see her feet. She wore a white nightgown or dress and seemed to glow from within, but the most amazing thing about her was her eyes. She had vibrant blue eyes that looked so sad. She smiled softly at him.

Suddenly, the general heard his wife coming from the bathroom. He glanced at his wife to get her attention. When he looked back, the girl was gone. His wife slowed down and looked at him keenly. "What's wrong?" she queried. "You look like you have just seen a ghost." The general looked back at where the girl had been only seconds earlier. "I think I just might have," he said.

The next day the general drove back from Pittsburgh to tell his story to the owner of the Jean Bonnet, and her staff gave him my phone number. He called me and told me his story. He was adamant about what he had seen.

The young mistress is not the only spirit said to haunt the Jean Bonnet. The first death known to have happened on the site also created the first ghost believed to haunt the building. In the fall of 1758, British general John Forbes was assigned to meet up with forces going westward to help take Fort Duquesne from the French. According to Forbes's papers, he paused at the old French fort five miles west of Bedford (probably the first floor of the Jean Bonnet Tavern) to wait for reinforcements to catch up with him. During that time, his men bivouacked in the woods near the old fort while the commander and his officers stayed inside the fort. At that time the French and British were vying for control of the region and each were paying people to spy for them. Teamsters and wagon masters were on the road and it was easy for them to get information about troop movements. While Forbes was ensconced at the old fort, his officers noticed that a particular wagon master was asking a lot of questions about troop movements. According to a local legend, the officers became suspicious and one night they had the wagon master brought into the fort to be questioned. It is said he confessed, was tried for treason, was sentenced to hang, and was executed all in one night. The body was then buried in the dirt floor of the old fort to make sure that the men did not find out that their troop movements could have been compromised.

The story has been passed down through the years, and it is said that in 1957, the then owners of the building dug up the floor during restorations and found the skeletal remains of a male. The bones predated the American Revolution and the man's neck was broken. Though the story of the spy and the skeletal remains in the floor cannot be conclusively proven to be connected, the two do seem to be part of the same event.

People have reported seeing a man in rough colonial clothing sitting at the table not far from where the body was found. The staff at the restaurant knows that in that room there is a table where the place settings are constantly being moved around. Busboys and waitresses have been startled by setting the table and turning away for only a second to find that all the silverware has been pushed into the middle of the table.

During the colonial period, the second-floor tavern was used to host a monthly circuit court. During one of those sessions, a man charged in, screaming that the Indians were after him. He begged the gathered assembly to protect him from the Shawnee who were not far behind. He said that they wanted him for horse theft but he claimed to be innocent.

The very idea of angry natives pouring into the tavern was enough to spur the memory of a man standing at the bar. The man was a traveler from Carlisle and he watched the exchange between the possible horse thief and the court. The court's dilemma was that they didn't want to have a problem with the natives and they didn't want to turn over the fellow either. They knew what would happen to him if they did. Suddenly, the man from Carlisle spoke up. "I think I know this fellow," he said, pointing to the possible horse thief. "He's the fellow wanted in Carlisle area for horse thieving. I seen him when he was caught down that way. He escaped and musta come up here. He's definitely a horse thief."

Based upon that testimony the horse thief was tried, sentenced, and hung in the building within a couple hours. Outside, the natives were amassing. They demanded that the horse thief be turned over to them. They had been stalled while the trial was underway. After the hanging, the horse thief's body was presented to the natives as proof that whites enforced the laws for everyone.

The horse thief is said to haunt the building today. A shadowy figure has been seen in the second-floor hallway and on the stairs on occasion. Some guests recorded EVP on the second floor near the stairs and captured a male shouting, "Get it off me!" Was it the horse thief still reliving the last moments of his life?

There are two rooms and two double-bedroom suites that can be rented at the inn on the third floor of the Jean Bonnet Tavern. After the bar and restaurant shut down in the evening, the bed and breakfast guests are left alone in the building. The bar is caged off, but otherwise the guests can move freely between the second and third floors. On several occasions the guests have experienced ghostly events.

Guests have reported rocking chairs moving on their own, the showers running when no one is in them, personal objects being moved or put away, and feeling or hearing people in the room when no one could be seen. There are other stories, however, that are truly amazing.

A few years back, a local beer distributor decided to make his son's first year of buck season special. He rented a suite at the Jean Bonnet and invited a hunting buddy to come along. They checked in the night before buck season began. They went to dinner, rode around to the site where they were going to be hunting the next morning, and then returned to get some rest. They had been told that the bar would shut down around 9 P.M.

The men fell asleep, but the beer distributor awoke in the middle of the night because he was very thirsty. As he sat there, he heard the sounds of an active bar from the floor below. He glanced at the clock and felt a little irritated. It was far beyond the time when the bar should have been closed, and yet it was still open. He sighed and stood up. With the bar still open, he decided to go down and get a glass of orange juice. He pulled on his jeans and a shirt and headed to the stairs. As he walked down, he heard the music and saw the lights. At the foot of the stairs everything suddenly stopped. The music, the clink of glasses, and the sound of voices dissipated, and the lights all went out. The doorways were blocked by the metal grates that they locked each night and the place looked abandoned.

The beer distributor ran to the windows overlooking the parking lot and saw that his was the only car in the lot. He stood there puzzling about what had happened for a few seconds. Was he dreaming?

The beer distributor returned to his suite and found his friend and his son were both also awake. They had heard the sounds of the nightlife in the bar, too. They listened to the beer distributor's story but could not explain it.

The current owners, Shannon and Melissa Jacobs, have had their experiences, too. Melissa runs the business end of things and one day she was in the second-floor office before the business had opened for the day. She was busy working when suddenly she caught herself getting up. She had been hearing the sound of a baby crying and, as a mother, had been responding to it before her conscious mind registered the fact. Melissa stopped and listened to the sound. It was coming from the third-floor guest rooms, but she knew that she was alone in the building. She would hear the baby crying on many other occasions and eventually got curious about it. One day the former owners stopped in, and Melissa worked the conversation around to the subject of the permanent ghostly inhabitants. She asked if they had heard anything odd. Both admitted that they had experienced phenomena from time to time. The wife piped up and said that what she heard most often was a baby crying on the third-floor guest area.

Through the years there have been many ghostly stories. Guests and staff alike have had experiences. One former staffer admitted that when she opened up, she often heard footsteps, like a lady in high heels, walking around the restaurant level behind her. It was unnerving to her. One morning she had come in and started a load of laundry while she began the prep work for the day. She returned to the back area to put the laundry in the dryer and hurried back out front to continue preparing for the lunch rush. Eventually, she remembered the laundry in the dryer and went back to fold the linens before they wrinkled. To her surprise, the linens were already neatly folded and stacked atop the dryer. She was alone in the locked building at the time. She simply thanked her invisible helper and continued on with her day.

Old Bedford Village

Old Bedford Village is an open-air historical museum located in Bedford County and consisting of approximately forty structures. The majority of the buildings are log cabins that were moved from other sites, log by log, and reassembled at the village site. To complete the historic village, other replica buildings were added, including a church, a general store (outfitted with shelving from a real store), a blacksmith's shop, and a jail.

Completed in 1976, the year of the American Bicentennial, the village sits on the remnants of an old farm. After the village's construction, archaeological digs revealed that the farm previously had been home to an older Native American culture. Remnants of the Monongahela group were discovered on the site, indicating a village existed at some point between 1250 and 1600. Archaeologists have also found artifacts from another more mysterious Native American group they called the Shenks Ferry culture.

Old Bedford Village offers the public a unique opportunity to experience lifestyles and structures of the colonial period, as well as special event weekends featuring reenactments of French and Indian War battles and demonstrations of spinning yarn, blacksmithing, and various other tasks from the time.

Although not well known, the very first ghost story to be associated with Old Bedford Village occurred shortly after the museum first opened. A costumed female docent was assigned to the Egolf farmhouse that sits back from the other houses. The docent wandered away to talk to another docent in the main part of the village. She saw a family headed toward the Egolf farmhouse and tried to excuse herself from her talkative companion. By the time the docent got free, a couple minutes had elapsed. She hurried down the path to the farmhouse and stepped inside to greet the family.

"I'm so sorry that I wasn't here to tell you about the house when you first came in," she gushed.

The husband smiled at her. "That's okay. The gentleman took us through and told us about the house." The man looked around, but the "gentleman" he was referring to was nowhere to be seen. Puzzled, the man looked back at the docent. "I can't understand it, he was just here."

The wife shrugged and pulled one of her little daughters closer. "He must have gone out the back door," she suggested.

The docent blanched and hurried to the door. All she saw was an open field. No one was there. She gathered her composure and turned back to the group and began to do her job; however, she could not help the tiny shudder that ran through her. There should have been no costumed men working in the village that day, so who had they seen?

Through the years, other odd events have occurred. In the winter months, Old Bedford Village can be rented for private events and reenactments. Many of the groups have made comments about certain homes.

One of the most interesting hauntings at Old Bedford Village is that of Christ Church. People often rent the church for weddings, and it was a woman decorating for a wedding who first mentioned that there was something unusual about the church. The church is a replica of the Union Log Church in Schellsburg, a few miles up the road. It has a central aisle leading up to the altar and a raised pulpit that the minister mounted by way of a set of stairs. There is a loft accessed from stairs in the back of the church. The small entry hall has a bathroom on the left as you enter, and it was there that the woman had her experience. She was decorating the church for a wedding the next day when she took a moment to use the facilities. While she was sitting in the stall, she heard footsteps approaching and looked down. She saw heavy, old-fashioned boots going by. Suddenly, the woman felt apprehensive and remained very quiet. She quickly finished up and eased her way out of the stall. No one was in the church and no one had opened the door to step outside. Frightened, the woman later mentioned it to the director at that time. He made light of the experience.

Later on, other people confided similar stories to the director. Two women decorating for another wedding also encountered a man in old-fashioned clothes who walked past them in the church and disappeared near the pulpit.

A male reenactor climbed up into the pulpit one night and was aping a minister. Suddenly, he felt as if the air was electric. Despite the fact that his friends were watching him, he hurried down the stairs and refused to go close the pulpit and altar again. He swore that someone was angry with him—a man whom he called "the deacon."

Still other people have encountered the spirit that has become known as "the deacon" while in the church. Some people see him or hear him walk by, and others sense that he is watching them and caring for the church. In 2011, a paranormal group visited the museum and a group of four ladies sat in the church snapping photographs in sequence. One of the women caught a black apparition moving through the church in a series of photographs. The apparition seemed to be crossing the back of the church.

There is another spirit who has been seen or sensed in the church—that of a little girl. Those who have seen her describe her as about six years old with blonde hair. Although the church is not known to have hosted any funerals, the child has communicated to sensitives that she is waiting where she last saw her body.

Of course, the church does sit near where the original farmhouse had once stood. Is the child from the farmhouse or did she come to Christ Church in some other way?

The same paranormal group came on another evening, and on this night a couple with several children was assigned the church. The man went up to the balcony where the little girl was most often seen and sat down. He talked to the spirit, although he didn't see anyone. He told her that he had brought her a teddy bear. He set a stuffed bear down in the seat in front of his own. He told the child about his own children and asked the girl if she would like to have the bear. Suddenly, he felt a coldness seep around him and he shivered. He sat perfectly still and watched as the teddy bear began to move slowly. No one was near and there was no air or other explanation for what was happening, but the bear was moving. First it slipped sideways to the left, and then straightened itself. Next, the bear moved to the right and fell over. The man picked up the bear and told her that it was okay, she could have it. He left the bear for her. No one seems to know what happened to the bear after that.

There are other houses in Old Bedford Village where activity has occurred. The Semanek house is described in the literature as an "old log mansion" and was built by Dr. William Smith prior to 1800. The house was originally located near the village of Ryot in West St. Clair Township. It belonged to Smith, who held a doctorate in divinity and was also a surveyor from Philadelphia. He purchased twenty-five hundred acres so early in the history of Bedford County that there are no written records to record the exact date. In 1802, Smith deeded a parcel of the land to his son, an attorney from Lancaster County. The house is named for its last owner, Allen Semanek, who dismantled it and donated it to Old Bedford Village.

Two local psychics have encountered a distressed woman in the house. She told both of them independently that she had taken up residence in the house after her husband had been killed by natives on his way to Ligonier. She said that she had come to the house to live with her sister after she had been widowed. On other occasions, voices have been recorded in the house speaking English and a language that might be Native American.

There are two schoolhouses in Old Bedford Village. The first one is the Knisely School House and it sits on the lower side of the village. It was built in 1869 by George M. Knisely on his farm near Pleasantville. The house remained in the Knisely family until it was donated by Mrs. J. H. Knisely in memory of her husband, Dr. Joseph Knisely, who had attended the schoolhouse. After it was no longer used as a schoolhouse, it was rented out as a private one-room house.

One evening, a woman was working in the schoolhouse when she suddenly felt the air change. Despite the fact that it was a sultry summer night, she was freezing cold. She stood up, as if ready to run, because she felt that was not alone in the room. She sensed a little boy about nine years old was there and he was trying to communicate with her. The woman's friends came to see how she was doing with her work and found her sitting there crying. They were very concerned and persuaded her to leave the building. They assisted her out and she slowly began to calm down.

The other school building in Old Bedford Village is known as the Eight Square School. The design is Quaker and legend has it that the building was designed in a circle with eight points so that the Devil could not pin the children in a corner and make them misbehave. But there were practical reasons why an eight-point building would work on the frontier. The desks for the older children were positioned to face out the windows rather than to look at the teacher. The design allowed the older students to look outward in case there was an Indian attack.

Paranormal investigators have recorded the sounds of children laughing and the sound of scraping desks and chairs. There is also a story of a former headmaster who has been seen in the doorway of the schoolhouse.

The Williams cabin also has been active in the past few years. The history of the Williams cabin is a bit confusing, because it was actually built on a piece of ground where three tracts of land came together. Each tract belonged to a different person, so it is difficult to say which family actually owned the cabin. It is known that the cabin originated in the Cumberland Valley and local documentation indicates that it was built in approximately 1776. There is an indication that the cabin was built by Thomas Coulter for his slaves. The 1772 census does indicate that Thomas Coulter was one of only two men in Bedford County who did own slaves; however, the old records are confusing and incomplete. The records for the cabin indicate that Daniel and Catharine Frey owned the cabin in 1804. There is no written tax record for the cabin prior to 1804. Furthermore, there are no tax records to indicate that anyone owning the cabin ever paid a slave tax. This means that either Thomas Coulter built the cabin before the written records in that area, or the records are incomplete.

Reprinted in the second volume of *The Papers of Henry Bouquet* is a letter Colonel Bouquet wrote to George Washington on July 14, 1758, to request "the assistance of your second company of artificers to build to Logg houses half Way. . . About 2 miles north of Centerville, Cumberland Valley Township, Bedford County, on a small ridge running North from the Bortz Church." The cabin did come from that area, and local people confirmed that the cabin known as the Williams Cabin did have a twin at one time.

There is little doubt that the cabin is one of the oldest in the county. It has had many owners, and on several occasions reenactors have reported hearing footsteps upstairs when no one was there and feeling unwelcome in the upper floor of the house. On three different occasions, a paranormal group has recorded EVP of a man on the second floor telling them to "Get out!" "Go away!" "Out!" On the first floor a young woman has been encountered. She seems intimidated by the male on the second floor.

During a charity event in 2011, a tourist captured an image on camera on the second floor of the blacksmith shop. Voices have been recorded in the event barn and on the lower level of the building as well.

Perhaps one of the strangest stories is of the sighting of a lady in a red shawl. It is a story that is persistently mentioned by visitors to the village. A reenactor named Dee Bishop posted a query on the website *Pennsylvania Mountains of Attractions* asking if visitors to Old Bedford Village had seen the mysterious lady. The post is followed by multiple comments from visitors who have seen a woman in a red shawl in the village.

In her post, Bishop wrote about a young teenage boy who left camp to take a morning walk. "When he returned he asked if we saw a woman all hunched over wearing a bright red shawl carrying a pitchfork and a bag. We all said no." The boy said that she walked past him and went into the woods. When he looked up, she had disappeared. According to Bishop, the boy "stated he didn't hear her footsteps on the leaves or ground. It was weird. It was pouring rain and no one was dressed in period clothing in that we were all leaving early." In subsequent comments, other visitors to the village claim to have encountered this woman in a red shawl. A former special events coordinator for Old Bedford Village stated that he had spent many nights in the village houses with various reenacting groups. He wrote, "You can see a lady holding a candle looking out the window on the top floor in House Two" (the Kegg-Blasko house). He also states, "I have also seen the lady with the red shawl."

Baker Mansion

Baker Mansion in Altoona is a thirty-five-room Greek Revival–style house that was completed in 1849 and originally owned by ironmaster Elias Baker. Today, it is the home of the Blair County Historical Society. Baker's family consisted of his wife Hetty, sons Sylvester and David Woods, and daughter Anna. The family had lost a daughter, Margaretta, when she was very young.

David Woods Baker married and had a daughter. Sylvester and Anna never married. Anna was the last of the Baker family to live in the mansion. She died in 1914, and after that the house was closed. In 1922, the Blair County Historical Society leased the house as a museum and headquarters for the society, and by 1941, they were able to purchase the property.

Baker Mansion contains many pieces of the Baker family's furniture, including the sofa on which Sylvester died. In the dining room is the War Governor's table, where the loyal war governors met to vow support for President Abraham Lincoln's plans during the Civil War. The second floor is filled with artifacts ranging from war memorabilia to children's toys. No longer on display is a wedding dress donated by the Bell family. The dress is believed to be haunted.

Two Bakers are said to haunt the mansion—Anna and Sylvester. Many of the paranormal events reported are attributed to Anna.

As a girl, Anna fell in love with one of her father's workers. When she showed her father the engagement ring and told him about the marriage, he became furious. Elias drove off the young man by telling him that Anna would be cut off from her family if they were ever married. He told the young man that Anna was unprepared to live such a rough life. Some folks speculated that the boyfriend was bought off, but there is no evidence of that.

Anna told her father that if she was forbidden to marry the young man, she would never marry at all. She fulfilled her promise. Anna has been seen walking down the main stairs of the mansion by staffers when they are alone in the building—and the doors are locked.

In 1981, *Life Magazine* featured the Baker Mansion as one of the nine most haunted houses in America and recounted the story of the haunted wedding dress. The dress belonged to Elizabeth Bell and was donated by the family to the historical society. Legend has it that Anna moves the dress as she dreams of a wedding that never took place. At one time, the dress was on display in a large glass case, along with a parasol and white slippers. The case had two locks on the back that required two different keys. People claimed that the dress swayed and the parasol and slippers switched places on occasion.

In recent years, it was revealed that one of the prior curators was a bit of a prankster who may have embellished the story to help generate interest in the mansion. The fact that the dress stopped moving after she left lends credence to the notion. Today, the internet is filled with speculation on why the dress is no longer on display. According to the historical society, the reason is because the dress is aging and fragile. They hope to have a replica made and displayed in the future, but for now the dress is being protected from further damage.

That said, when *Life Magazine* staffers visited Baker Mansion, they spoke to the *Altoona Mirror* newspaper about the difficulties they had photographing the dress. "We have experienced an incredible amount of problems working on this story. We have had our baggage and cameras arrive late several times, including today," said the photographer who accompanied the article's author, Rosemarie Robotham. The photographer expounded on the problems they had photographing at Baker Mansion. "The strobes had always worked perfectly before. When we set up to begin shooting, neither of them worked. We couldn't get them to operate despite all our efforts, so we had to dismantle both and use parts from each to shoot." Perhaps someone didn't want that wedding dress photographed after all.

Another mysterious story involves a mocking knock. One evening, a young woman from out of town ran out of gas on the quaint back road that runs behind the mansion. She saw lights in the mansion and decided to go inside to ask to use the phone. In the darkness she did not see the museum sign and thought that she was going to a private dwelling. It was late and the sight of lights in the windows was most welcome. The young woman knocked on the back door and waited. Suddenly, someone inside the house knocked back. She waited a moment but the door did not open. She knocked again and once more someone inside knocked back. She got angry because she felt that the person inside was mocking her. She left, vowing to return in the morning and give someone a piece of her mind.

The next day the young woman did return. This time, she saw the museum sign. Still, someone had been inside who had not helped her. She rang the bell and the curator opened the door. The young woman stepped inside and told her story. She asked who had been on duty the night before. The curator hesitated before responding. "I'm sorry but we close at 5 P.M.," the curator explained. "I know that no one was in the building last evening. I was the last person to leave and that was about 5:30 P.M. I locked up and the building was empty." The curator neglected to say that the house was haunted, but she had to be thinking of the mansion's reputation.

Sylvester, too, is said to be visiting his earthly home. He lived most of his life in the mansion. As an elderly man, he often rested on the sofa in the "single parlor," which was more comfortable and informal than the room known as the "double parlor." One evening a relative sat reading to Sylvester while he reclined on the sofa. He stood up to go to bed and paused a moment. Suddenly, Sylvester fell to the floor before the sofa and died of a heart attack.

In the 1980s, a new security system was installed in the building. Pressure pads were laid down under the carpets. When the system was activated, the pads would detect movement and notify the police, indicating the exact location of the movement. On multiple occasions, the security pads went off in the single parlor in front of the sofa when the building was locked up at night. In fact, one night the pad over the spot where Sylvester died was literally crushed. The technician who replaced it said it looked like someone had fallen on it.

One night the alarm went off and the police officer who responded brought along his K-9 trained German Shepherd. The dog rushed into the house and began to sniff around for a prowler. The police officer led the dog toward the single parlor, because the dispatcher said that it was the alarm in that room that had gone off. At the doorway to the single parlor, the dog froze, backed away, and turned to run out of the house. No amount of coaxing could induce him to enter the single parlor. That same experience would be repeated twice more through the years. Was Sylvester reliving his moment of death?

The Regina music box in the single parlor is also said to play by itself. Through the years, the box has spontaneously burst into life for a few seconds. Perhaps Sylvester winds the box because no one else usually does.

Mary in the Attic

The names of those involved in the story were changed to protect their identities. When the Addison family moved into their new home in Altoona, they were thrilled. They had long dreamed of having a large old house where they could raise a family, and the white clapboard home at the end of the street in their Altoona neighborhood seemed to be just that place. They were practical people, so ghosts were the last thing on their minds. In fact, they had many other things to be concerned about—Rachel Addison was about to give birth to their first child.

The little girl, Lisa, came on a cold winter's morning and they were thrilled. They brought their baby back to the white clapboard house and settled down. Although they tried to have other children, it just did not seem to work out. Still, they had Lisa, and for them that was enough.

Lisa grew into a lovely and lively young girl. By the time she was four years old, she was all elbows and knees and long dark hair. She already knew her ABCs and had begun to learn to read. She was a sponge soaking up the world around her, and her parents were thrilled.

When Lisa turned six, she suddenly had an invisible friend. At first, the Addisons smiled indulgently at their little girl and her invisible friend, whose name was Mary. Lisa talked freely about her friend, and that soon made her parents concerned.

Lisa told them that her friend Mary lived in the attic. She was sixty-eight years old and had died up there. This was not the kind of imaginary friend they had thought Lisa would have. They had expected a little girl who would keep their daughter company for a few weeks and then go away like most imaginary friends do. But Mary did not go away, and she became more of an influence in Lisa's life as the girl grew older.

Lisa's parents were uncomfortable talking about Mary, but Lisa would share bits and pieces of her conversations with Mary. She told them that Mary had told her the house had once been a double house and that Mary had lived on the second and third floors of that house. Mary said she had baked bread for a living and sold it out of the first floor, along with pies and cakes. She called her business a bakery.

When the holidays rolled around again, Mary had stories to tell about that as well. She talked about decorating her living room, which was now the master bedroom, and about how she had loved to make the house beautiful for the holidays. Mary told Lisa that she had been in the attic to fetch Christmas decorations when she had climbed on a chair to reach a box and had fallen. She struck her head and lay there injured for a while. Then Mary said she had a sharp pain in her chest and down her arm and everything went black. When Mary woke up she could see her body lying on the floor, but she could not get back inside her body.

As time went on, Lisa's parents began to discourage her from talking to Mary. They were growing increasingly uncomfortable with what they were thinking. Rather than being the typical imaginary friend, was it possible that Mary was a ghost?

Lisa's grandmother, Paula, was not as put off by Mary has Lisa's parents were. Paula decided that if there were any truth to this story she would find it in the historical society or the newspaper morgue. Paula set off on a quest to discover if there really was a Mary, and if her history of the house was accurate.

It took several trips to the historical society before Paula found that she was looking for, but when she saw the papers she felt her heart flutter. In the 1940s, the house where Lisa lived had been the Capano Bakery.

Paula discovered that there were still members of the Capano family in the Altoona area. She made several phone calls and found the grandchildren of the Capano family, who had once run a bakery from the house. She explained that her daughter had purchased the house and that they were looking into the history of the property. She wondered if anyone might have photographs or stories to tell about the house.

Janet Capano James agreed to meet with Paula. She said she had stories to tell about the house and some photographs of her grandmother's that she could share with the family.

Paula asked her to the home and the two ladies settled in for a nice visit. Janet explained that when she was a little girl, her grandfather and grandmother, Ralph and Mary Capano, had started a bakery on the first floor of the house and moved their residence to the second and third floors. After Ralph passed away, Mary continued to run the bakery, although she needed some help from her children to keep it going.

In 1977, the bakery was shut down but Mary continued to live on the second floor. The third-floor attic had been returned to storage and Mary rarely went up there because she had arthritis in her legs that pained her most of the time. However, one day in early December Mary decided to climb the stairs and bring down the

Christmas decorations by herself. She loved Christmas, and decorating for the holidays was her favorite part. She had dragged three boxes to the doorway and returned to the attic for yet another box when she had her mishap. She had stored a box of decorations on top of an old closet, and she pulled an old chair over in order to climb up and lift the decorations down safely. Throwing caution to the wind, Mary had climbed up on that chair, and then must have lost her balance. She fell hard and landed among the boxes of decorations. Mary struck her head and lost consciousness for a while, according to the coroner. She suffered a fatal heart attack while lying in the attic among the decorations that she had so treasured.

According to Janet, it was the next owner who had returned the first floor to living quarters and removed every trace of the house once having been a bakery. Then, Janet held out an old photo album and began to flip through it. She showed Paula pictures of Mary and Ralph standing in front of their bakery, and close-ups of Mary throughout the years. The last photograph was of Mary only approximately a year before her death. Paula realized that what her granddaughter had experienced was not an invisible friend, but rather a friendly ghost. She requested a copy of Mary's last photograph so that she could show it to Lisa.

Paula received the copy of the picture a few days later and showed it to Lisa. Lisa smiled and nodded. "That's a good picture of Mary," she said.

When Lisa was eight years old, the house was severely damaged when a car struck it. Lisa's parents decided it was time for them to move, as it would have been cost prohibitive to rebuild the old structure. They broke the news to Lisa, who began to cry. "What happens to Mary?" she asked. "If you tear down her home, where will she go?" Honestly, her parents had not thought about that.

After much discussion, it was decided that they would tell Mary the truth and ask her to come with them. Lisa's parents had come to accept Mary as a part of their lives, and now they didn't want to be responsible for abandoning her.

On the last Saturday before the move, Lisa, her mother, and Grandma Paula gathered in the attic. They talked to the room, hoping Mary would be listening. They explained the situation and then asked Mary to come with them. There was no response that they could see, but they felt as though she had listened to them.

Three days later, the move was complete. It took about a week to tear down the house, and a couple more weeks to clean up the mess. The family wondered all along if Mary was still in the house, but they had no way of knowing.

About a month after the house had been torn down, Lisa awoke one Saturday and came bouncing down the stairs. She was grinning from ear to ear. "Mary is here," she announced. "She was in my bedroom this morning. She says that this is a nice house and that she has missed me."

With that, Mary came to live with Lisa once more. Lisa is now in her late teens and still Mary visits her from time to time. Perhaps Mary is slowly slipping away so that Lisa can live her life, but she can't seem to stay away completely. When Lisa is sick or sad or alone, Mary comes with her sweet smile and talks to her even now.

The Legend of Lakemont

Nestled in Central Pennsylvania is Blair County, a sprawling region with many wonderful tourist sites. One of the most famous is Lakemont Park. The land where the park now sits was donated by the once-prominent Baker family for the amusement of the citizens. Before that there were ore furnaces on the land. Today, Lakemont Park is the eighth oldest amusement park in the nation. The park opened in 1894 as a trolley park, but by 1899, it had become an amusement park.

One attraction at Lakemont is Leap-The-Dips, the oldest working wooden roller coaster in the world. Installed in 1902, Leap-The-Dips is today a National Historic Landmark.

Leap-The-Dips is also locally famous for another reason. It is said to be haunted. Although the story has never been officially acknowledged by the Lakemont Park staff and owners, the story refuses to die.

According to local lore, a maintenance worker was killed during a test run of the new roller coaster. The worker had been working on the track and was struck down by the roller coaster because he didn't realize that it had been set in motion for a test run before opening the ride.

Through the years, occasional riders have seen a man working on the track as they take their joy ride. The coaster nearly strikes the man and it shocks the tourists so much that they take the time to mention it to the ride driver or to park management. They are usually reassured that no one was working on the track at the time, and so they could not have seen this man; however, many of the tourists are insistent that they did see someone on the track.

The Strange Tale of the Dick Family

Harmon Dick was of Scottish descent. Born in 1756 in Scotland, he immigrated to Hesse Castle, Germany, where he became part of a company of Hessian soldiers hired by the British government to come to America to squash the colonial uprising. Harmon was a big man at six foot two inches and weighing 253 pounds. He was considered quite a soldier and fought with honor for the British until he was captured.

Christmas 1776 found Harmon Dick in Trenton serving under Colonel Johann Rahl. The night was bitterly cold and the Delaware River was blocked with ice. The British and Hessians made the mistake of underestimating General George Washington and his Continental forces. They expected him to stay put in Pennsylvania through the holiday; however, Washington managed to cross the river and fight a victorious battle in Trenton.

One of the men captured by the Continental Army in Trenton was Harmon Dick. He stood out among the other captives. Like the other prisoners, he was given the opportunity to swear allegiance to the American government, which he did

Harmon became a Federalist and settled near Roaring Spring, Blair County, where he raised a large family. Their oldest child was named Jacob. In 1786, when Jacob was in his early teens, a terrible epidemic spread through the area. The first person struck down by the disease was Jacob. He grew steadily more ill and then died. For the next fourteen years, the epidemic continued. Not a family in the area was left without deaths in the family. In fact, it got so bad that some people wondered if the illnesses would continue until no one was left.

When people gathered, they talked about the strange illnesses and about how they had all lost loved ones. One night, people began to talk about how the illnesses had begun. Jacob Dick had been the first one to die. Someone suggested that the illnesses were not natural. Perhaps the illness had something to do with Jacob Dick.

A group of citizens decided that maybe by exhuming the body of Jacob they might figure out what was happening. They went to the little cemetery where Jacob was buried and exhumed the body.

They pulled the casket from the ground and pried the lid off the coffin. Inside they saw a shocking sight. The teenage boy's corpse was fourteen years old but still intact. The boy's hair was snow white and long, and he had a long white beard down over his chest. As they stared in horror at the corpse, it suddenly began to break apart, turning to dust. The people closed the casket and reburied the body. After that, the illnesses stopped. Those who were already ill quickly grew well again. Harmon and his wife named their youngest baby son Jacob, in memory of the boy they had lost so long ago.

What happened in that long ago village just outside of Roaring Spring? Did a curse or plague infect a family and town? The strange story from the Dick family leaves more questions than it answers.

The Old Cambria County Jail

The Old Cambria County Jail looks like an old Welsh castle sitting formidably in the center of Ebensburg, Pennsylvania. The sandstone structure was built in two sections, with the oldest section dating to 1872. The prison was built to relieve the pressure of the smaller first prison housed in the basement of the courthouse.

When the prison opened in 1874, it had thirty-four cells and these soon filled up. Through the next few years, the prison was kept full and often took center stage in local dramas. In all, there would be eleven hangings in Cambria County, nine of them at the Old Cambria County Jail. The hangman's platform still exists within the jail itself and has been enclosed in a glass showcase. Other displays exhibit prison life, including shanks fashioned by prisoners and several hangmen's ropes actually used in executions.

One of the men hanged at the prison was Charles Carter, who died on April 9, 1890. He had been convicted of murdering his friend and was told that he would not need an attorney; he was consequently found guilty. Some of the hangings at the prison were big events, requiring tickets to get in. The hanging of Stephen Fellows and Jacob Hauser was such an event. The two men were executed at 1:30 P.M. on February 15, 1906, and they met their maker before a packed audience. It is said that people scaled the walls of the prison yard to watch the event.

Beneath the prison is the area called the "dungeons." The dank rooms are a hodgepodge that today is the domain of pigeons and bats, but at one time it was used as housing for prisoners. There are iron rings in the walls that indicate that people might well have been chained down there in the damp darkness. It was probably used to detain troublemakers or the mentally ill. An addition was built onto the prison in 1911 and that added fifty-two cells. The new cells were soon filled, too. The newer section was warmer than the older section and slightly nicer, but a jail is still a jail. In 1997, a new prison was built and the Old Stone Jail was retired. Today, the new section is used for records storage by Cambria County and the first floor of the old section is the museum. Guests are not allowed on the second or third floor or in the warden's quarters on the third floor. Guests, likewise, are not allowed to enter the basement.

The last warden to run the prison reputedly had a paranormal experience in the old section of the prison. He was having a meeting with his staff on the first floor in the hallway. As he spoke, he and the guards became aware of a figure on the third floor on the narrow walkway. The person was male and appeared to be wearing a prison uniform. The warden ordered his guards to split in two. One group, led by him, would go up the metal stairs to the third floor. The other group would mount from the only other set of steps, effectively cutting off the prisoner. They would pin him between the two groups and capture him. The prison is structured for maximum visibility, and a person can see from the first floor up through the second and third. The warden and his men began the maneuvers to pinch the prisoner between them. They reached the third floor walkway from both sides. As the two groups moved down the aisle toward the man, he simply vanished. The warden later said that was when he realized that they were chasing a ghost.

In addition to the hangings, many other prisoners, of course, died there. In the last years of the prison's active use, a prisoner in the new section slit his wrists so that he could get out and see his wife who was a nurse in the local hospital; however, he was not found in time and bled to death. His cell was removed to make way for a bathroom for the records staff. It is believed that he returns to relive his last few desperate minutes. People have reported hearing a man crying or moaning in that area.

The prison hosted murderers and criminals of every ilk. Most of the ghosts there are sad fellows or people still looking for a way out.

The Miracles of Prince Gallitzin

The people of Loretto still revere Father Demetrius Augustine Gallitzin. Known as the Apostle of the Alleghenies, he is so well-regarded that many members of the Catholic community there believe he should be made a saint. There are several accounts of miracles attributed to him.

Gallitzin was born an aristocrat on December 22, 1770, in The Hague, the son of Prince Demetrius Alexeievich Gallitzin, the Russian ambassador to the Netherlands, and Princess Adelheid Amalie Gallitzin, born of a great German family. At the age of seventeen Prince Dmitri converted to Roman Catholicism, and in 1792, he went to America, where he entered the priesthood. This decision displeased his father, who cut off his inheritance.

Father Gallitzin was the first priest to receive all degrees of holy orders in America. He was a member of the Order of Saint Sulpician and saw his life as playing out in studious retreat from the world. In the spring of 1796, Bishop John Carroll received a message from a Mrs. Burgoon of the Maguire settlement (present-day Loretto) asking for a priest to come and hear confession for a woman who was dying and wanted to become a convert before she left the earth. Bishop Carroll sent Gallitzin to hear the confession and assist the dying woman. It would be Father Gallitzin's first foray into the Allegheny Mountains.

Gallitzin suddenly had a vision of a Catholic colony in the Allegheny Mountains and when he returned to Baltimore, he sought permission from the archbishop to be permanently assigned to the sparse population of Western Pennsylvania. Carroll happily granted him permission, asking Gallitzin to build up a four-hundred-acre tract of land that had been bequeathed to the archdiocese years earlier by the Revolutionary War captain Michael Maguire. Gallitzin returned to the Maguire settlement and made it his home. He built a small log chapel to service the few Catholics already in the area. He served his congregation but also continued his quest of building a Catholic colony.

Gallitzin purchased large tracts of land around the Maguire settlement so that settlers would come to his area and put down roots. He believed that this was the way to create his colony and eventually, a Catholic nation. He either sold the land at huge discounts or gave land away to those willing to settle there.

Throughout his lifetime, Gallitzin denounced the damage that was being done to families by the sale of alcohol in his community and he spoke out against it from the pulpit. His words carried great weight in Loretto and those purveying alcohol saw a decrease in demand for the substance; they blamed Gallitzin. Angrily, the alcohol purveyors denounced the priest and threatened his life and his church. One night, a group of drinkers and those who made their livelihood from drink gathered together and in a drunken moment decided to teach the priest a lesson. Everyone in Loretto knew that the father valued nothing more than God, his chapel, and his congregation. The drunken mob decided to burn the chapel as a lesson to the priest, and if he were there they would strike him dead as well.

Passions burned high in the town and a group of Catholics saw the mob headed for the chapel. The Catholic men rushed forward to protect their priest and their church. Gallitzin tried to calm the mob with his words, but to little avail. One of the men shouted him down and another screamed that they should burn the church. In

the melee that ensued, a man struck at Gallitzin, but one of his parishioners threw his arm up to protect the priest and took the blow himself. That night the Catholic men saved both their church and their beloved Father Gallitzin, but for the man who saved Gallitzin there was a price to pay. His arm was severely damaged and he was never able to lift it or use it again.

For the rest of his life, Gallitzin maintained a special friendship and bond with the gentleman. Gallitzin never forgot the blessed act of kindness that had protected him from harm that night long ago, nor the fact that his friend carried the memory of that event in his useless arm.

When the gentleman died, the injured arm assumed the position it had on the night when it absorbed the blow meant for Gallitzin. No one could straighten the arm to put it into the casket and so they had to accommodate it when they buried him.

Years later, the family would decide to move the gentleman to another local cemetery where the rest of the family was buried. When they did so, they disturbed the casket and it broke open. To everyone's surprise, although the rest of the corpse had decayed normally, the arm that had saved Gallitzin from harm had not decayed at all. It was as fresh and fully formed as it had been on the day when the gentleman had been buried. This was looked upon as a miracle and a sign that Gallitzin was a saint. At the little chapel that still sits beside the cemetery where the corpse is buried, there is a stained-glass window that depicts the uncorrupted arm of this gentleman.

Another miraculous story associated with Gallitzin is that of a stranger. According to Gallitzin's writings, he was extremely concerned over the financial straits of his church. Because Gallitzin purchased plots of land that he either sold at less than market value or gave away, this was a burden upon him. At one time Gallitzin found he was unable to pay his bills because anticipated funds failed to materialize. He was distraught over the situation and prayed a great deal about this. He was not sure how God would provide, but he was certain that God would meet his need as he always had in the past. One day, a stranger came to Gallitzin's door asking for food. The good father brought the stranger in and gave him a meal. The two men passed a pleasant afternoon speaking, and the stranger seemed comforting to Gallitzin. The priest found himself discussing his financial worries with the man. The stranger comforted him and assured him that God would answer his need in his own time.

Eventually, the stranger stood up to leave and thanked Gallitzin for the food and companionship. Gallitzin walked the stranger out the door and then turned back into his house. On the table close to where the stranger had been sitting was a little pouch that Gallitzin had not noticed before. He grabbed the pouch and ran out the door to give it back to stranger. Although the time had been too brief for the stranger to be gone, he had vanished.

Gallitzin walked up and down the road but could find no trace of the stranger. Puzzled, he took the pouch back inside and opened it. Inside was the exact amount of money that he needed to pay off his debts. Gallitzin would come to believe that God had sent an angel to meet his needs.

In Loretto, there are people who believe that Gallitzin has not left his congregation behind. There are stories of church members doing maintenance inside the building and seeing an elderly priest near the altar. Those who have seen him turn around say it is the visage of Father Gallitzin. An elderly woman who used to press the vestments for the priest insists that on several occasions she encountered Gallitzin while working in the church.

Elmhurst

Elmhurst estate sits near the little town of Cresson in Cambria County. It was built as a summer cottage for the Thaws of Pittsburgh. At the turn of the twentieth century, the Thaw family was one of the wealthiest families in the nation. They made most of their fortune by investing in railroading. The summer cottage at Elmhurst was a twenty-three-room English Tudor mansion surrounded by an orchard and acres of woods. The Thaws spared no expense when building Elmhurst. European woodwork gave way to imported wallpapers and opulent furniture. Elmhurst was a fine example of how the upper crust lived in the early 1900s. The Thaws hosted their social equals, authors, and people from all phases of the arts. Perhaps one of the most famous, or rather infamous, women to ever stay at Elmhurst was Evelyn Nesbit Thaw.

Evelyn Nesbit was born Florence Evelyn Nesbit in Tarentum, outside of Pittsburgh, on December 25, 1884. Her father was an attorney who never made much of his practice. Her parents doted on her, and later on her little brother as well. When Evelyn was eleven years old, her beloved father died suddenly. The little family was left penniless and homeless when all their worldly goods were sold to meet the outstanding bills. The family was in dire straits and lived in a series of one-room boarding houses as Mrs. Nesbit struggled to find work.

Eventually Mrs. Nesbit found work as a seamstress, but it was sporadic at best. She was advised that she could find steady work in Philadelphia, so they moved. Mrs. Nesbit picked up sewing work with some theater folk, but also took a job at Wanamaker's Department store as a clerk. Now Evelyn was fourteen years old and her brother was twelve. Both of the children soon were also employed at Wanamaker's, working long hours for little pay.

Evelyn was a beautiful young lady and her looks were about to change her life. One day, a female artist approached young Evelyn and explained that she wanted to hire her as a model. Mrs. Nesbit agreed to allow Evelyn to pose for the woman. Evelyn earned a whole dollar. Her combination of innocence and coy sensuality attracted the interest of other artists. Evelyn was soon posing for several artists in the Philadelphia area. She quickly realized that she could earn more money modeling than working in a store. Evelyn's sultry looks put her in demand.

Mrs. Nesbit was in a quandary because well-bred young women did not model for artists and photographers, but Evelyn wanted to model and the money was sorely needed. The Nesbit family moved to New York City so that Evelyn could continue to pose for more artists and photographers. Mrs. Nesbit later said that she was careful of Evelyn's reputation and never allowed her to pose nude, but nude and partially nude photographs have been found. Evelyn posed for *Vanity Fair*, *Harper's Bizarre*, and *Ladies' Home Journal* and became the darling of advertising. She posed for everything from toothpaste to Coca-Cola. She modeled for tobacco cards, suggestive postcards, and calendars. Evelyn would become the first pin-up girl. Eventually Evelyn would capture the eye of Charles Dana Gibson, who immortalized her as one of his Gibson Girls.

Despite the fact that Evelyn was making more money than her whole family had once earned, they were still having financial difficulties. New York City was an expensive place to live, and Evelyn began to focus on the theater as a new source of income. Promoters recognized the potential of having the famous model in their shows. The Broadway manager of the Floradora Girls made Evelyn an offer, and she pushed hard for her mother to accept it. She moved on from there to do other Broadway plays, including *The Wild Rose*, which cemented her reputation and brought her great acclaim.

Mrs. Nesbit's was concerned about Evelyn's reputation but she also knew that some young theater girls caught the eye of millionaires who married them. Evelyn had long ago become the sole bread winner for her family and it was in everyone's best interest that Evelyn should succeed.

Evelyn's great beauty caught the eye of millionaire architect Stanford White. White, a married man, was known for his philandering ways; in fact, he kept a private apartment above a toy store for his mistresses. The opulently decorated apartment featured a red velvet swing, which fascinated young Evelyn.

Forty-seven–year-old White set about wooing sixteen-year-old Evelyn and succeeded. Evelyn did not stand a chance against such a wealthy and powerful man.

White realized that the way to Evelyn's heart was through her family. He moved her family into the opulent Wellington Hotel. White presented himself to Mrs. Nesbit as a friend and a man who was taking a fatherly interest in Evelyn. He paid for Evelyn's brother to go to school and generously paid for Mrs. Nesbit to return to her hometown to visit family and friends she longed to see. He volunteered to chaperone young Evelyn himself.

A couple days after Mrs. Nesbit left on her trip, Stanford White invited Evelyn to dine with him at his apartment. That evening, he allowed Evelyn to have champagne and took her on a tour of the apartment. Evelyn later stated that she remembered nothing after the tour until the morning, when she awoke naked in bed beside "Stannic." White and Evelyn had just begun an affair. Evelyn certainly recognized that Stanford White's protection was a blessing in her life. Their relationship was odd in many ways. White doted upon her as if she was his daughter in some ways, and yet he had a passion for young Evelyn that he indulged carnally.

Eventually, Evelyn began to date other men. Among her conquests was artist and illustrator John Barrymore (later the famous actor of stage and screen). When Mrs. Nesbit and Stanford White found out about the relationship, they were both angry, but for different reasons. White was jealous and Mrs. Nesbit was distressed because Barrymore's income was not enough to keep Evelyn and her family in the style to which they had become accustomed. White broke up the relationship by paying to send Evelyn to a boarding school. Before Evelyn was whisked away, Barrymore asked her to marry him, but Evelyn turned him down.

John Barrymore was not the only man that Evelyn had been seeing at the time. She dated several other men, including young Harry Thaw. Harry Thaw was one of the wealthiest men in the nation and was from Pittsburgh, not far from where Evelyn had been born. Thaw's family made their money in coal and railroading, but young Thaw was a troubled man. He had struggled with mental illness since childhood. As an adult, he got away with his shenanigans because of the Thaw family name. Now, Thaw was enchanted with Evelyn and pursued her doggedly. Like White, he realized that wooing Evelyn would require befriending her family, and so he contrived to not only meet Evelyn but also to get to know her mother.

Near the end of her relationship with Barrymore, Evelyn suddenly underwent a surgery. It was speculated that she had an abortion, but officially it was announced that she had appendicitis. After the surgery, Thaw convinced Mrs. Nesbit that a trip to Europe was just what poor Evelyn needed to lift her spirits and help her heal. Mrs. Nesbit agreed as long as she could accompany the young couple as a chaperone.

Thaw had promised a slow and gentle journey, but it was anything but that. He was known for running full tilt and that is exactly what he did. Evelyn grew weaker physically and mentally. Worse yet, Evelyn and her mother fell out over how Thaw was treating them. Evelyn saw him as her champion and Mrs. Nesbit had begun to distrust the rich young man. Mrs. Nesbit wanted to return to America, but settled for being allowed to stay in London. She was too old for the frightful pace of Harry's trip. Evelyn continued on to Paris.

Throughout their relationship, Harry had repeatedly enforced for Evelyn his personal obsession with female chastity. As Harry began to press Evelyn for her hand in marriage, she felt that she needed to tell Harry the whole truth. Finally, in Paris, she laid bare the truth of her relationship with Stanford White. She explained about the night when she had lost her virginity and how she believed that Stannic had drugged her or the champagne had gone to her head.

Thaw was livid. He knew White and his reputation and repudiated the man's character. Thaw questioned Evelyn mercilessly, but he was gratified to see that Evelyn was shamed by her own willful conduct that had placed her in harm's way. As Thaw saw it, Evelyn had been betrayed twice. First, by her greedy mother who had allowed a wolf to have access to her daughter, and then by Stanford White, the wolf, who stole Evelyn's virtue. When Evelyn tried to defend her mother, Thaw flew into a rage.

Thaw seemed even more obsessed with virginity and visited sites dedicated to virgins during the remainder of the journey. He wrote scathing and illogical vitriolic comments about Stanford White in a visitor's book at the birthplace of Joan of Arc in France.

From France, the couple went to Austria, where Evelyn's life would be forever altered. Thaw had rented a castle for their stay, but he ordered the servants to stay in anther wing. He and Evelyn inhabited one wing alone. There he literally locked up Evelyn and suddenly his personality changed. Thaw began physically and sexually abusing Evelyn daily. He beat her with a whip and inflicted great pain. He seemed to enjoy her pain and Evelyn feared that he would not release her. But two weeks later, the trip continued on. Thaw apologized for raping and torturing her and seemed to consider the matter closed. To Evelyn's shock, Harry Thaw seemed genial and happy, as if their sojourn in the castle had allowed him to rest.

When Evelyn made it back to society, she confided her tale of horror to some friends. Only then was she told of Harry's darker side. She was not the first person he had beaten and raped. There were stories of maids who were abused by him and even of a young bellman who had been mistreated. Several male friends warned her that Harry had an addictive personality and that he did morphine. Evelyn realized that she was in a bad situation. Having her name linked to so many wealthy men had given her a reputation that was making steady work hard to find. That was further complicated by her illness and long absence from the stage to travel with Harry through Europe. Worse yet, Stanford White was still part of her life, but she had come to realize that she would never rise above the rank of mistress for him. Evelyn was angry with White for not warning her of Thaw's reputation. She was feeling very alone because she and her mother had not been able to patch up their disagreement, and her mother had since remarried, which only served to further separate them.

Harry Thaw had pursued her for nearly four years. He continued to find ways to meet her and he obsessively attended her shows. He showered her with gifts, begged her forgiveness, and blamed his ill-treatment on the drugs. He vowed that if she would marry him, he would give up the drugs and change his life. He would prove to her that he could be a good husband and gentle man. Thaw explained that it was the stress of her revelations that had caused his aberrant behavior, but that he had forgiven her for being seduced by White.

Evelyn knew that her chances of marrying a millionaire had dwindled and Harry Thaw was the only man asking to marry her now. Thaw had become the very vision of gentleness with Evelyn, and she finally agreed to marry him. His family agreed to the marriage under the condition that Evelyn cut all ties with her former world. Her time as a model, actress, and mistress would be blotted out.

Evelyn married Harry Thaw on April 4, 1905, in a strange ceremony. Harry had insisted that he pick Evelyn's wedding dress and in keeping with her role of fallen woman he had her dressed in black. Afterward, newspapers proclaimed Evelyn "Mistress of Millions," and perhaps Evelyn consoled herself that she would be mistress of a fine home and a fortune and for that she could tolerate Harry's moods. But if that was her idea, then her life did not go as planned. Harry took Evelyn back to Lyndhurst, the family mansion in Pittsburgh, where his mother, Mary Thaw, ruled with an iron fist.

Mrs. Thaw was a very religious woman who subjected Evelyn to her own strict beliefs. Evelyn found herself in a group of people who were very much like "Mama Thaw," as she was instructed to call her mother-in-law. Thaw seemed content with things and joined in with his mother and her friends. He went after Stanford White with puritanical zeal. He was determined to ruin the man who ruined his wife. Thaw joined reformers who wanted to clean up the social scene and became a reformer himself. It was at that time that Harry Thaw began to carry a gun. He became convinced that Stanford White had hired a gang to kill him, so Harry felt justified with being armed.

For his part, White paid little attention to Harry Thaw. He called him a clown, but never took Harry seriously. If he had any qualms about Evelyn's marriage, he never voiced them publically and moved on with his own life. There were new conquests to be had and young maidens to woo. Not only that, but also there was work to be done. White was one of the most famous architects in the nation at the time and justifiably so. He had designed many grand churches and public buildings throughout New York and the nation. He even designed the second Madison Square Garden, which was hailed as a marvel.

Pittsburgh in the summer was not something that the social elite had to suffer through. The smoke, the dirt, and the smells were all too much for the refined to deal with, and they retired to their "summer cottages" in the central part of Pennsylvania. Elmhurst was the summer residence for the Thaw family, and Evelyn was taken there early in the spring.

Things had been bad in Pittsburgh, but at Elmhurst they got worse. Harry was giving frequent vent to his more base urges. Away from the need for social propriety, Harry could feed his dark need to hurt. Evelyn was beaten, sexually abused, and made miserable at Elmhurst. She was isolated and Mama Thaw was willing to turn a blind eye to Harry's abuse as long as it didn't affect her socially. In her later years, Evelyn Nesbit wrote a biography in which she discussed how much she hated her visits to Elmhurst.

After weeks at Elmhurst, Evelyn convinced Harry that they should make a journey to New York City. To her relief, he finally agreed, despite the fact that it was where the dreaded Stanford

White resided. With Evelyn's return to New York came the rumor mill. Gossips said that Evelyn Nesbit had returned to New York to see Stanford White. They gossiped that the two were resuming their torrid affair, and some even claimed that the affair had never really ended. Evelyn knew of Harry's pathological hatred for White and she had to be careful to not even mention him or his friends to Harry.

On the evening of June 25, 1906, Harry and Evelyn met friends at Madison Square Garden for a play. The Nesbits were in town only briefly while Harry planned another overseas trip and he had surprised Evelyn with a night out. The show was premiering at the rooftop theater, and Evelyn, Harry, and his two male friends were enjoying the show. Despite the heat, Harry insisted on keeping his long black dress coat on throughout the evening.

About 11 P.M., Stanford White entered the theater and took his place at his reserved table. He seemed to pay no attention to Evelyn or her party. Thaw had been acting strangely all evening. He had been restless and got up repeatedly through the performance. Once he saw White enter, he grew even more agitated. Evelyn also noticed White and began to ask if they could leave.

Thaw's friends knew the situation and that their friend had an unpredictable temper. They encouraged Evelyn's idea of leaving as the show was just ending. Much to Evelyn's horror, Harry got up several times and walked toward White, only to turn back. At last, he agreed to go and they made it to the elevators. There he paused and instructed Evelyn to go down without him. He said he had left something on the table and needed to retrieve it. Harry turned back, walked up to White, pulled a gun, and shot White three times in the face. White dropped to the ground and Harry stood over the body. He held the gun aloft and addressed the stunned crowd. His exact words varied depending on the witness, but he reportedly stated something like "You ruined my wife." People were not sure if this was part of the performance or not, and there was stunned silence for a few seconds. Harry turned and, still carrying the gun high, exited to join his wife still waiting at the elevator.

Evelyn saw the gun in Harry's hand and heard the noise behind him. "What have you done?" she breathed. Harry looked at her calmly. "I have probably saved your life."

Suddenly pandemonium reigned. People realized that this was not part of the show and everyone wanted to get out. Police officers arrested Thaw and Evelyn slipped away unnoticed in the crowd. She was stunned as she heard what had happened.

What ensued was a circus of a trial. The first trial ended in a hung jury and the second trial ended with the verdict of "not guilty by reason of insanity." Throughout the trial, Evelyn's life and morals were the real question. Thaw's defense was that he had killed the man who had wronged his wife. Every relationship Evelyn had ever had was called into question. She was left destroyed and unable to find work in the United States. Eventually, Evelyn had to move to Europe to find employment and support the infant son she had with Harry. Mama Thaw had cut Evelyn off without a penny after she was no longer needed to testify for Harry. The marriage was dissolved and Harry would live in a comfortable suite at the prison where he was incarcerated. It was furnished from his home; he had a butler, a chauffeur, and traveled often.

Evelyn died on January 17, 1967, at the age of eighty-two in California, where she had made her home finally. In 1942, Lyndhurst had been razed, so Evelyn's spirit was never associated with that house, but at Elmhurst things were different. Elmhurst had been sold to the Westminster Presbytery of Pittsburgh prior to Evelyn's death. At the time of Evelyn's death, a young couple named Hoover had been hired to be caretakers of the estate. The property was to be used as a retreat for the church. A house trailer was placed on the property for the Hoovers and their three small children to live in.

Not long after moving into the trailer, the Hoovers began to notice something strange. When they went to bed at night someone or something would turn down their thermostat, so that they awoke to a cold house. The Hoovers could not explain how or why the thermostat was being turned down. The children were too young to know what it was and too small to reach it. They had not turned it down, so who had?

Late one night, Mrs. Hoover was lying in bed thinking about her plans for the morning when she heard footsteps in the hall. She followed them mentally, expecting them to stop at the bathroom, but they continued down the hall past her bedroom. She could hear the

steps passing by, but she could not see anyone attached to the sound. Thus began a strange sort of haunting. There were disembodied footsteps, doors that banged, knocking without anyone there, and even a disembodied male voice that called out Mrs. Hoover's name on occasions when she knew that she was alone in the trailer.

One night Mrs. Hoover was restless, tossing and turning, and unable to get comfortable. As she turned over to face the wall, she froze in fear. Between her and the wall, a gauzy column of mist was forming. The mist took the shape of a human and she was positive that it was man. She reached over to shake her husband awake, but by the time she roused him, the mist had dissipated. Later she would begin to question what she had seen and confessed that she was not sure any longer that the misty figure was male. The more she thought about it, the more she began to believe that it was the shape of a woman wearing a wide brimmed hat.

The trailer was not the only part of the property thought to be haunted. As the Hoovers came to know too well, the main house, Elmhurst mansion, was actually the center of the paranormal activity. The Hoovers spent much of their day inside the house cleaning and doing repairs. They began to notice that even though they turned the lights out each evening when they left, the lights would turn themselves back on for morning. At first they thought that this was a practical joke and decided to keep the lights on that night. The couple watched the house until bedtime, leaving the lights on when they went to sleep. No one had a key to the house other than themselves and the clerics from their church. To their surprise the next morning, every light have been turned off.

Throughout their stay on the property, they found that certain phenomena occurred again and again. On countless occasions, the lights turned themselves on or off, they would find the front door standing open despite having locked it securely, stove burners would turn themselves on, and furniture would be moved about the house when it was locked and empty. When they were alone in the house, they would hear footsteps or the sound of loud knocking on the walls and doors. At times it got so bad that Mrs. Hoover insisted that she would not stay in the house alone.

The house was used extensively during the spring, summer, and fall, but in the winter the Hoovers spent a great deal of time on the property alone. They tried to explain away the phenomena, but it grew difficult when the lights began to turn themselves on and off in front of them. They began to suspect that the spirits haunting the house were attempting to make contact with them.

At the time, they knew very little of Elmhurst and its history. They only knew that it was a beautiful old mansion their church owned and that they greatly enjoyed working there. There were times, however, when Mrs. Hoover was particularly unnerved. She would feel so frightened on occasion that she would flee the house and stay in the driveway until her husband returned. One day, she was in the kitchen cooking when she felt someone touch her. As she turned, she heard a man clearly call her name and she realized that she was not alone in the house. On other occasions they felt watched. They felt as though there were people standing just beside them whom they could not see, and there were cold spots that moved through the house and passed by them.

The Hoovers made a decision early on to not speak about what was happening at the house. They did not want to be considered unchristian. They, likewise, did not want to frighten their children with ghost stories. As time went by, the Hoovers began to hear stories about the old Thaw mansion. Locals occasionally told them stories about the house and the Hoovers began to understand that others knew about the haunting. Finally, the Hoovers began to confide in close family and friends some of what they were experiencing.

One day, a couple drove up to the mansion house and asked if they might go in. Mrs. Hoover struck up a conversation with the couple as they toured the house and learned that these people had once been caretakers at the mansion; in fact, the Hoovers had replaced them. Suddenly, the Hoovers realized that here was an opportunity for confirmation of what they were experiencing. They began to steer the conversation toward the unusual. Mrs. Hoover finally asked if anything mysterious had ever happened in the house or on the grounds while the former caretakers had been in residence. The former caretaker's wife laughed and said, "Goodness, we were here for nearly four years. Many a night my husband got up with a shotgun thinking someone had gotten in." The former caretakers confirmed that they, too, had problems with the lighting, doors opening and closing, pounding and knocking, footsteps, disembodied voices, and being physically watched and touched.

The Hoovers loved Elmhurst and considered it a privilege to be able to work there. They did not feel that the spirits in the house meant them any physical harm, so they decided to continue working as caretakers.

On several occasions family or friends came to the house to visit, not knowing that the Hoovers had left for the day. Later on, their friends or family members would mention that they had stopped by to ask about the beautiful young woman in a long white dress whom they could see standing in the hallway. The young woman seemed distressed by their knocking and rather than answer the door, she would walk past it and disappear into the depths of the house. The young woman was always described as very beautiful and petite with dark hair piled atop her head and a slightly sad or frightened look on her face. The Hoovers knew that the young woman was not flesh and blood, but they did not yet have a name to the face.

Mrs. Hoover decided that she needed to learn all that she could about the history of the property so that she could understand the haunting better. She took a trip to the local historical society, where she learned a great deal about Elmhurst. As she flipped through the thick file on Elmhurst, she was struck by the pictures of beautiful young Evelyn Nesbitt and her darker, brooding husband. Mrs. Hoover read the story of all that had happened to young Evelyn, and of what had transpired within the house. She found out that Evelyn had died in southern California only shortly before people began to see the beautiful young woman in a white dress. She learned that Evelyn had disliked Elmhurst because of the isolation and abuse she was subjected to at the house. Mrs. Hoover came to believe that the young woman in white was Evelyn Nesbitt, but she wondered why Nesbitt returned a place she had hated in life. She also began to suspect that the male entity who had frightened her might be Harry Thaw.

One day, Mrs. Hoover was preparing food in the kitchen for a retreat group that was to arrive in a few hours. She had brought her young daughter with her and the child was contentedly coloring at the table while chatting with her mother. Suddenly, the little girl yelped in pain. The stool the child was sitting on tipped over and she struck the floor, spilling crayons as she went down. Mrs. Hoover rushed to her child to comfort her, but the child would not be quieted. She insisted that someone had pulled her hair. Mrs. Hoover reasonably pointed out to the child that they were alone in the kitchen, and that she had been across the room at the time when she had fallen.

There was simply no one in the room who could have pulled the child's hair. Somewhat mollified, the little girl scrambled back up into her seat and her mother picked up the crayons and handed them to her. The child began to color again. Mrs. Hoover kept a watchful eye on the little girl while she prepared the retreat dinner. Suddenly, her daughter cried out as the stool toppled again. This time Mrs. Hoover had seen the child's hair being roughly tugged just before the stool had tipped. The little girl insisted that again someone had pulled her hair hard and that they had pushed the stool over. Mrs. Hoover did not try to rationalize the second experience. She merely turned the stove off and took her daughter outside to wait until someone else arrived.

Another afternoon, Mrs. Hoover heard a car pulling up outside the mobile home and went out to greet the young woman. The young woman was a teenager named Julie who explained that she was doing a history paper for school on Elmhurst. She asked if it would be possible to take a tour and some photographs to accompany her report. Mrs. Hoover was exhausted from having hosted well over a hundred people for the entire weekend, but she agreed to take the young lady through the house. Julie assured her that she would not take up much of Mrs. Hoover's time, and they drove up to the main house together.

Inside the house, Mrs. Hoover began to feel nervous. She had never before felt as though she was intruding in the house, but suddenly she had a terrible feeling that they had to leave the house immediately. She rushed through the tour of the first floor while struggling to not run out of the house. She started up the stairs to the second floor while explaining about the historical importance of the house. A wave of fear washed over her, and she knew that they had to get out of the house right away. She glanced around fearfully but saw nothing that should have frightened her. Still, the feeling was swallowing her up and she turned to Julie and said, "We need to get out of here now."

Julie followed Mrs. Hoover as she rushed down the stairs without asking what was wrong. It was as if a panic gripped both of the women and they broke into a run as they descended the stairs and headed for the front door. Outside, both women regained their composure, and Julie asked if she could take a photograph of the front of the house. Mrs. Hoover nodded and Julie took a Polaroid camera from her car and snapped a picture. She laid the picture on the backseat, where it could develop, and thanked Mrs. Hoover for allowing her to tour the house.

Mrs. Hoover would probably not have thought anything more about her experience with Julie if Julie had not returned a week later. She brought the Polaroid photograph back with her and handed it to Mrs. Hoover. It was a shot of the front of the house showing the porch, the front door, and the floors above the front entrance. Julie insisted that Mrs. Hoover look closely at the photograph and tell her if there was something wrong with it. Mrs. Hoover looked from one window to the other as she examined the picture, and her breath caught in her throat. There was a face peering out from the third window on the second floor. The face was white and almost looked like a mask, but there was no question that something or someone had been watching them that day.

Julie brought the picture back because she was hoping that Mrs. Hoover could explain to her who the figure in the window was. Mrs. Hoover had no explanation. Julie's father would later have the photograph enlarged and sent to Polaroid, asking if they could determine what had happened to create this image on the film. The Polaroid lab stated that it was not a fault in the film nor was the photograph touched up. Julie's father took an 8-x-10 copy of the photograph and gave it to the Hoovers.

Eventually, the church decided that rather than repairing the mobile home, they would create a caretaker's apartment on the third floor of the house. This meant that the Hoovers would be living in Elmhurst all of the time. The church wanted to remove the mobile home and make the Hoovers more accessible to the retreat guests. The Hoovers had little doubt that they would continue to experience hauntings, but they also loved the house so much that they believed it would be worth it.

Not only did the Hoovers experience the hauntings, but some of the retreat guests also did as well. Usually the Hoovers played off the sound of footsteps, pounding in the walls, or the feeling of being watched as just part of the ambience of an old house.

Through the years, the Hoovers began to differentiate the personalities of the ghosts who haunted the house. The man seemed to be the prankster who made the sound of footsteps and pounding and called out their names. The young woman, who they believed was Evelyn, seemed to appear as she had looked when she had lived in the house. They thought that she was trying to warn them that something evil was in the house and that they should take care. They believed that this evil entity was the one responsible for giving people a feeling of terror. If there was anything about the haunting that truly disturbed them, it was the moving of furniture, the physical touching and pulling, and the sound of a couple eternally fighting up on the second floor.

Eventually the church decided to sell the estate, and the Hoovers were devastated by the notion of having to leave. They finally decided to go into a partnership with some friends and buy Elmhurst. It was large enough to be a restaurant and bed and breakfast. The partners decided that the Hoovers would remain in residence on the third floor.

The Hoovers lived in the house from 1969 until the early 1980s. They consider their time at Elmhurst to have been a blessing. They freely admit there were times when they were disconcerted or even frightened, and that their experiences certainly were beyond normal, but Elmhurst was special for them. Mrs. Hoover treasures her time at Elmhurst both for its history and for its hauntings.

Today, Elmhurst has passed through a series of private owners. It has been altered, although it still retains its grandeur and is a home once more. There are times when the house quickly passes from one owner to the next and stories circulate through Cresson that owners are still having experiences. But it is difficult to say if the house is still being haunted by Harry Thaw, Evelyn Nesbit, and others. One can only speculate that a house that has been so consistently haunted probably does still retain some of its spirited inhabitants.

Bibliography

Books and Articles

"Atrocious Murder." *Philadelphia Inquirer*, March 1, 1889, p. 8.

Anthony, C., trans. *Cincinnati Commercial Tribune*, January 22, 1887.

Fell, Cassandra, and Walter L. Powell. *Ghosts and Legends of Fort Ligonier*, 2008.

Guiley, Rosemary Ellen. *Ghost Hunting Pennsylvania*. Cincinnati: Clerisy Press, 2009.

Hull, Laurie. *Supernatural Pennsylvania*. Atglen, PA: Schiffer Publishing, 2010.

Liberace. *The Wonderful Private World of Liberace*. Paducah, KY: Turner Publishing, 2003.

Nesbitt, Mark, and Patty A. Wilson. *Haunted Pennsylvania: Ghosts and Strange Phenomena of the Keystone State*. Mechanicsburg, PA: Stackpole Books, 2006.

———. *The Big Book of Pennsylvania Ghost Stories*. Mechanicsburg, PA: Stackpole Books, 2008.

Reevy, Tony. *Ghost Train!: American Railroad Ghost Legends*. Lynchburg, VA: TLC Publishing, 1998.

Salaz-Marquez, Ruben. *I am Tecumseh!*. Book II. Alameda, NM: Cosmic House, 1985.

Skinner, Charles M. *Myths and Legends of Our Own Land*. Vol. I. Philadelphia: J. B. Lippincott, 1896.

Swetnam, George. *Pittsylvania Country*. New York: Dell Publishing, 1951.

———. *Devils, Ghosts, and Witches: Occult Folklore of the Upper Ohio Valley*. Greensburg, PA: McDonald and Sward, 1988.

Swope, Robin. *True Tales of the Unexplained*. Erie, PA: Open Gate Press, 2010.

———. *Eerie Erie: Tales of the Unexplained from Northwest Pennsylvania*. Charleston, SC: History Press, 2011.

Tampani, Beth E. and Charles J. Adams III. *Ghost Stories of Pittsburgh and Allegheny County*. Wyomissing, PA: Exeter House 1994.

White, Thomas. *Forgotten Tales of Pennsylvania*. Charleston, SC: History Press, 2009.

——. *Forgotten Tales of Pittsburgh*. Charleston, SC: History Press, 2010.

——. *Ghosts of Southwestern Pennsylvania*. Charleston, SC: History Press, 2010.

Wilson, Patty A. *Haunted Pennsylvania*. Laceyville, PA: Belfry Books, 1998.

——. *The Pennsylvania Ghost Guide*. Vol. 1. Roaring Spring, PA: Piney Creek Press, 2000.

——. *Monsters of Pennsylvania: Mysterious Creatures in the Keystone State*. Mechanicsburg, PA: Stackpole Books, 2010.

——. *UFOs in Pennsylvania: Encounters with Extraterrestrials in the Keystone State*. Mechanicsburg, PA: Stackpole Books, 2011.

Wilson, Patty A., and Scott Crownover. *Boos and Brews: A Guide to Haunted Taverns, Inns, and Hotels of Pennsylvania*. Roaring Spring, PA: Piney Creek Press, 2002.

Wudarczyk, James, Jude Wudarczyk, Allen Becer, and Daren Stanchak. *A Doughboy's Tale and More Lawrenceville Stories*. Pittsburgh: Lawrenceville Historical Society, 2004.

Websites

"5 McKean Slayers Have Paid Penalty." *Painted Hills Genealogy Society*. http://www.paintedhills.org/Most_Wanted/mckeanslayers.htm.

"13 Bends." *Ghost Hunters and Occult Spirits Team*. http://www00.homepage.villanova.edu/drew.schauble/bends.htm.

"13 Bends, Harmarvilla, PA." *Strange USA*. http://www.strangeusa.com/Viewlocation.aspx?id = 64179#sthash.0SedG6AX.dpbs.

"Altoona: Lakemont Park." *Forgotten USA*. http://forgottenusa.com/haunts/PA/10194/Lakemont%20park.

Bardsley, Marilyn. "The Kingsbury Run Murders or Cleveland Torso Murders." *trutv*. http://www.trutv.com/library/crime/serial_killers/unsolved/kingsbury/index_1.html.

"Bedford Springs Resort History." *Bedford Visitors Bureau*. http://www.visitbedfordcounty.com/springs/index.html.

Bishop, Dee. "Lady with the Red Shawl." *Pennsylvania Mountains of Attractions*. http://www.pennsylvania-mountains-of-attractions.com/lady-with-the-red-shawl.html.

"The Black Cross." *Steel Town Paranormal*. http://www.steeltownparanormal.com/index.php?p = 1_51.

Book of the Royal Blue. Baltimore: Baltimore and Ohio Railroad, 1906. From *Internet Archive*. http://www.archive.org/stream/bookofroyalblue11balt/bookofroyalblue11balt_djvu.txt.

Bibliography

Bulloch, Joseph Gaston Baillie. *A History and Geneaology of the Families of Bayard, Houstoun of Georgia, and the Descent of the Bolton Family from Assheton, Byron, and Hulton of Hulton Park.* From *Online Library.* http://www.ebooksread.com/authors-eng/joseph-gaston-baillie -bulloch/a-history-and-genealogy-of-the-families-of-bayard-houstoun-of -georgia-and-the—llu/page-3-a-history-and-genealogy-of-the-families-of -bayard-houstoun-of-georgia-and-the—llu.shtml.

"Commonwealth v. Crossmire." *Atlantic Reporter.* Vol. 27. St. Paul: West Publishing, 1894, p. 40–42. From *Google Books.* http://books.google .com/books?id = K8fzAAAAMAAJ&pg = PA41&lpg = PA41&dq = Ralph + Crossmire + Murderer + Pa&source = bl&ots = EXYLEnFaKG&sig = ZP3OBJeZbDFc1xGCx2QCkjEDpXg&hl = en&sa = X&ei = IrU3Uc2KBeqx0AHB5oDYBg&ved = 0CDcQ6AEwAg#v = onepage&q = Ralph%20Crossmire%20Murderer%20Pa&f = false.

"Crossmire." *Planet Smethport Project.* http://www.smethporthistory.org/ king.street/jail/crossmiremurder/crossmire.htm.

Davis, Shirley, and Robert Allen. "History of Anderson Family, Including Espy Family History and National House." Bedford County Arts Council, 2009. *docstoc.com.* http://www.docstoc.com/docs/133687083/Anderson -House-History.

Emerson, Sylva. "A Brief History of Blair County." *Blair County Historical Society.* http://www.blairhistory.org/graphics/BLAIR_COUNTY_HISTORY .pdf.

"Erie/I-80 Haunts and History." *Google Sites Haunts and History.* https://sites.google.com/site/hauntsandhistory/eriei -80hauntsandhistory.

Gibb, Tom. "Cambria County Jail Reopens as a Museum." *Post-Gazette.com,* January 6, 2002. http://old.post-gazette.com/neigh_east/20020106jail3 .asp.

"Grand Midway Hotel." *Pennsylvania Haunts and History.* http:// hauntsandhistory.blogspot.com/2008/05/grand-midway-hotel.html

"History of Bedford Springs, The." *Omni Hotels and Resorts.* http:// www.omnihotels.com/FindAHotel/BedfordSprings/OurHistory.aspx.

"History of Hill View Manor, The." *Hill View Manor.* http://www .hauntedhillview.com/History/History.html.

Ieraci, Ron. "Rolling Hills Asylum." *Pennsylvania Haunts and History.* http://hauntsandhistory.blogspot.com/#uds-search-results.

"Is Hill View Manor Haunted? Take a Tour and Find Out." *Elwood City Ledger,* October 28, 2011. http://www.ellwoodcityledger.com/news/local_news/ is-hill-view-manor-haunted-take-a-tour-and-find/article_c3d4e3cb-f130 -562e-8f78-1fafa75b161d.html.

Knortz, Karl. "American Folklore" *Folklore Historian* 5, no. 1 (Spring 1988): 14-42.

"Lakemont Park, Altoona, PA: The Haunted Roller Coaster." *Ghosts of Central Pennsylvania.* http://ghostsofcentralpa.blogspot.com/2010/10/ lakemont-park-altoona-pa-haunted-roller.html.

"Lawrence County Home (Hill View Manor)." *Lawrence County Memoirs.*
http://www.lawrencecountymemoirs.com/lcmpages/153/lawrence
-county-home-hill-view-manor-shenango-twnp-new-castle-pa.

Levine, Arthur. "Lakemont Park." *About.com Theme Parks.* http://
themeparks.about.com/od/findusthemeparks/p/lakemont-park.htm.

"Liberace's Midnight Visitor." *Pennsylvania Haunts and History.* http://
hauntsandhistory.blogspot.com/2009/02/liberaces-midnight
-visitor.html.

Lockhart, R. "Murder of Polly Williams." *USGenWeb Archives.* http://files
.usgwarchives.net/pa/fayette/newspapers/williams02.txt.

Long, Kody. "The 'Lady' That Crawls on the Wall." *Pennsylvania Mountains
of Attractions.* http://www.pennsylvania-mountains-of-attractions.com/
the-lady-that-crawls-on-the-wall.html.

"Martha." *The Grand Midway Hotel.* http://www.iliveinahauntedhotel
.com/Screening/Martha.htm.

Mellot, Kathy. "Building a Case for Sainthood: Couple Send Prince Gallitzin
Research to Vatican." *The Tribune Democrat.* http://tribune-democrat
.com/local/x175061825/Building-a-case-for-sainthood.

Mitchener, Charles Howell. "Legend of Louisa St. Clair, the Governor's
Daughter." *Historic Events in the Tuscarawas and Muskingum Valleys,*
1876. From *Clan Sinclair.* http://sinclair.quarterman.org/who/louisa/
index.html.

"Murder of Polly Williams, Fayette County, PA 8-17-1810." *Yahoo Groups:
Williams Cousins.* http://groups.yahoo.com/group/WilliamsCousins/
message/152.

"National Aviary." *Haunted Houses.* http://www.hauntedhouses.com/
states/pa/national_aviary.htm.

"Oil Region Ghost Story, An." *Yahoo Groups: PA_Legends.* http://groups
.yahoo.com/group/PA_Legends/message/1250.

Pellas, Dawn. "Daytrippin: Old Cambria County Jail." *WeAreCentralPA.com.*
http://wearecentralpa.com/fulltext?nxd_id=374492.

"Pennsylvania's 6th Most Haunted Place Is Smethport." *Welcome to
Smethport, PA,* September 19, 2008. http://smethportpa.org/news/
pennsylvanias-6th-most-haunted-place-is-in-smethport.

"Prince Gallitzin Attains First Rung to Sainthood." *Ridgway Record,* June 7,
2005. From *Catholic Answers.* http://forums.catholic.com/showthread
.php?t=59370.

Reabuck, Sandra K. "Borough Wants to Spruce Up Old County Jail." *The
Tribune Democrat,* September 26, 2012. http://tribune-democrat.com/
local/x354163168/Borough-wants-to-spruce-up-old-county-jail.

Sinclair, Fiona. "General St. Clair and His Descendants." *Fiona
Sinclair's Home Page.* http://www.fionamsinclair.co.uk/genealogy/
Isles/GeneralArthur1.htm.

Skinner, Charles M. "The Obstinacy of Saint Clair." *Read Book Online.*
http://www.readbookonline.net/readOnLine/58905/.

Bibliography

Stine, Rich. "Who Was Killed in the Midway Hotel in Windber, PA in 1949?" *Ask.com*. http://www.ask.com/answers/125684541/who-was-killed-in -the-midway-hotel-in-windber-pa-in-1949.

Summers, Ken. "Take Me Home, Zombie Roads." *Who Forted?* http:// whofortedblog.com/2011/09/26/home-zombie-roads/.

"Three Rivers Haunts and History." *Google Sites Haunts and History.* https:// sites.google.com/site/hauntsandhistory/threerivershaunsandhistory2.

"Twenty-Eight at New Home." *New Castle News*, November 4, 1926. From *Lawrence County Memoirs*. http://www.lawrencecountymemoirs.com/ lcmpages/638/lawrence-county-home-hill-view-manor-first-residents -article.

"Unlucky Engine, An." *Bathurst Free Press and Mining Journal.* June 28, 1890. *Trove.* http://trove.nla.gov.au/ndp/del/article/65348928.

"Washington County Pioneer News Stories." *Geneaology Trails History Group.* http://genealogytrails.com/ohio/washington/news_pioneers.html.

"Zombie Land." *Pennsylvania Haunts & History.* http://hauntsandhistory .blogspot.com/2008/06/zombie-land.html.

Acknowledgments

I WOULD LIKE TO THANK MY EDITOR AT STACKPOLE BOOKS, KYLE Weaver, and his assistant, Brett Keener. I also thank Marc Radle, whose artwork graces this book. Each of these people has touched the book and helped to shape it. I am grateful for their work and input.

I would also like to thank my sons, who have traveled with me and listened to my many stories. Thanks, guys.

About the Author

PATTY A. WILSON LIVES IN PENNSYLVANIA WITH HER FAMILY AND HAS been writing about the paranormal and folklore for more than thirty years. She is the author of *Monsters of Pennsylvania, UFOs in Pennsylvania, Haunted West Virginia,* and *Haunted North Carolina,* and coauthor with Mark Nesbitt of *Haunted Pennsylvania* and *The Big Book of Pennsylvania Ghost Stories.* Her articles have been published in *FATE* magazine and *Countryside.*

Other Titles
by Patty Wilson

Other Titles in the

Haunted Series

WWW.STACKPOLEBOOKS.COM • **1-800-732-3669**